BIRDS NESTING

By the late
J. G. BLACK.

SECOND EDITION.

ISBN 978-1-4067-9910-1

PREFACE

James Gavin Black was born at West Boldon, near Sunderland, not a very inspiring district for a boy who was destined to develop in after life a tremendous love for Nature in all her aspects. His father died when Gavin was only nine years old, but he was old enough to have imbibed some of his father's love of sport and of an open air life. He cannot be said to have inherited his taste for Natural History, but to have attained to it as so many others have done before him through his fondness for fishing and shooting. I believe his first introduction to fishing was on the Tees when his family stayed for a short time at Cotherstone, they afterwards went to live at Carperby and there he began fly-fishing in earnest on the Yore, a river much less frequented then by fishermen than it now is; so keen did he become that he has told me that he has been known to run down to the river on the morning of the opening day. In time he acquired great skill in fly-fishing, as indeed he did at anything he seriously took up, but it was always trout fishing and not salmon fishing that appealed to him most. While at college he took to shooting, though he never became a really first class game-shot, he knew more about the habits of game-birds than most gamekeepers or shooting men. He came to Corchester Preparatory School as a master on leaving Cambridge in 1902, and it was there that he first began to take up the study of birds as a serious hobby. The rest of his life was spent at Corchester, with the exception of an interval at Cambridge and another when serving during the War, until his sudden and unexpected death in August, 1926, at the beginning of the summer vacation.

The inception of the original of this book was somewhat haphazard; J. G. B. had always looked forward to taking up the threads of his work at Corchester as soon as he was demobilised and he had no reason to think that there was anything the matter with his health likely to prevent him from doing so, but a medical examination by the Army authorities told another story, and he was warned that unless he took a complete rest from all work for two years the consequences might be very serious. So the early months of 1918 found him at Corchester with nothing to do but eat, sleep and read, generally to lead an aimless existence. One day my wife said to him, "Why don't you write a book? A book about birds. Something to interest the Boys." The idea took hold and henceforth he again had an object in life. The book was begun in February and by the end of April it was practically complete, a publisher was found and terms arranged, but it was not until July that it was put before the public. Its reception was somewhat mixed, of course all Corchester boys at once bought copies and a number of copies were bought by other Preparatory School boys, but to many people the title was unattractive, they jumped to the conclusion that it was a book to encourage the systematic robbing of birds' nests by boys, instead of being what it is, a book to guide the love of birds' nesting innate in most boys into humane channels.

I cannot give readers of this book a better idea of the character of the author than by quoting from an obituary notice which appeared in the School Magazine, "The Corcestrian."

"It is rarely that one finds in one man so many and varied accomplishments. He never undertook anything unless he was prepared to do it as thoroughly as possible ; he had no use for second-hand knowledge, he liked to find and think things out for himself, he was a fine classical scholar, he went to Cheltenham College with an Entrance Scholarship, and went on to Caius College, Cambridge, with a Classical Scholarship ; he was a first class rifle shot and captained the Cheltenham College VIII. at Bisley ; he was a first rate field ornithologist and in his book, "Birds Nesting," he did his best to instil boys with some of his enthusiasm for birds and his wonderful skill in finding their nests. Botany was another of his hobbies, originally taken up with the object of giving boys another interest on their country rambles, and which later became an absorbing

PREFACE.

interest to him. He was also a good geologist and during his second period at Cambridge he selected this as the subject in which to take his Exam. and I have been told that had the University regulations allowed him to sit for Honours he would undoubtedly have obtained a first class. He was a keen fly-fisher and I believe this was the sport he loved most; he was never happier than when at the water side with a rod in his hand and it was a treat to see the skill with which he threw a fly over a rising trout. He was very fond of shooting, too, and for many years rented a small rough shooting in North Tyne, camping out on the moor often with two or three boys as companions; but both in fishing and shooting he cared more for overcoming difficulties—for catching fish when they were slow to rise, for outwitting birds when they were few and wild—than for heavy creels and big battues. He was an expert photographer and his photographic records of boys and events at Corchester have long been a unique feature of the life of the School. He was intensely musical and quite lately he devoted himself to introducing boys to some of the best music by means of the gramophone. He was one of the best and most painstaking Rugby Football coaches that any school could have, and a most patient and successful teacher of swimming."

If this edition of "Birds Nesting" should be the means of inculcating a humane love of birds in any young people, it will be the most fitting tribute to his memory that his former pupils could have devised.

G. S. S.

MARCH, 1929.

CONTENTS

Part I.
		PAGE.
How to set about it	....	1
1. What to take with you	....	1
2. Where to look	....	3
3. When to look	....	6
4. How to look	....	8
5. Climbing	....	17
6. What not to do	....	21
7. The egg collection	....	26
8. The note-book	....	28

Part II.

The birds, their nests and eggs, and their breeding habits	....	30
Introductory	....	30
Migration	....	31
Family I.—The Crows	....	35
Family II.—The Starlings	....	44
Family III.—The Larks	....	46
Family IV.—The Wagtails and Pipits	....	49
Family V.—The Finches	....	56
Family VI.—The Thrushes	....	72
The Warblers	....	84
Family VII.—The Dipper	....	98
Family VIII.—The Wren	....	99
Family IX.—The Flycatchers	....	102
Family X.—The Swallows	....	104
Family XI.—The Shrikes	....	107
Family XII.—The Tits or Tit-Mice	....	108

CONTENTS.

		PAGE
FAMILY XIII.—THE WOODPECKERS	....	118
FAMILY XIV.—THE CUCKOO	....	120
FAMILY XV.—THE KINGFISHERS	....	122
FAMILY XVI.—THE SWIFTS AND NIGHTJARS	....	125
FAMILY XVII.—THE EAGLES	....	128
FAMILY XVIII.—THE HAWKS	....	129
FAMILY XIX.—THE FALCONS	....	132
FAMILY XX.—THE OSPREY	....	135
FAMILY XXI.—THE OWLS	....	135
FAMILY XXII.—THE PIGEONS	....	142
FAMILY XXIII.—THE GAME-BIRDS	....	146
FAMILY XXIV.—THE RAILS	....	157
FAMILY XXV.—THE WADERS	....	165
FAMILY XXVI.—THE HERONS	....	183
FAMILY XXVII.—THE CORMORANTS	....	186
FAMILY XXVIII.—THE DUCKS, GEESE AND SWANS		188
FAMILY XXIX.—THE GULLS	....	197
FAMILY XXX.—THE TERNS	....	203
FAMILY XXXI.—THE PETRELS	....	207
FAMILY XXXII.—THE AUKS	....	209
FAMILY XXXIII.—THE DIVERS	....	213
FAMILY XXXIV.—THE GREBES	....	214
OBSERVATION	....	218
HAUNTS	....	220

PART III.

A BIRD'S NESTING CALENDAR 223

PART IV.

COLOUR INDEX 226
MYSTERIES 235

ILLUSTRATIONS

FIG.			
,,	1.—JAY	facing page	viii
,,	2.—RAVEN		1
,,	3.—CHAFFINCH		16
,,	4.—LINNET		17
,,	5.—YELLOWHAMMER		32
,,	6.—REED BUNTING		33
,,	7.—ROBIN		48
,,	8.—WILLOW WREN		49
,,	9.—WHITETHROAT		64
,,	10.—LESSER WHITETHROAT		65
,,	11.—BLACKCAP		80
,,	12.—SPOTTED FLYCATCHER		81
,,	13.—GOLDCREST		96
,,	14.—GREATER SPOTTED WOODPECKER		97
,,	15.—NIGHTJAR		112
,,	16.—NIGHTJAR SITTING		113
,,	17.—BUZZARD		128
,,	18.—SPARROW HAWK		129
,,	19.—YOUNG PEREGRINES		144
,,	20.—YOUNG BARN OWLS		145
,,	21.—BROWN OWL		160
,,	22.—WATERHEN		161
,,	23.—GOLDEN PLOVER		176
,,	24.—REDSHANK		177
,,	25.—WOODCOCK		192
,,	26.—CORMORANTS		193
,,	27.—EIDER DUCKS SITTING		208
,,	28.—TERNS		209
,,	29.—GUILLEMOTS		208
,,	30.—GUILLEMOTS		209
,,	31.—PUFFINS		224
,,	32.—LITTLE GREBE		225

FIG. 1—JAY
(see page 42)

Fig. 2—Raven

(see page 43)

BIRDS NESTING.

PART I.

HOW TO SET ABOUT IT.

§ I. WHAT TO TAKE WITH YOU.

Boxes.—If you mean to *collect* eggs, the first thing you need is a box; and the most useful box I ever had was a tin cigarette-box (100 size) divided into compartments with strips of cardboard. Each division was lined with cotton wool, and the lid covered with the same, so that all one had to do was to open the lid, slip the egg into an empty space, and shut it again, to have one's egg safely packed. Larger eggs than the box was meant for could easily be accommodated by pulling out a division and making two spaces into one. This is better than carrying a lot of little pill-boxes, as you are very liable to pull out one that has an egg in it already, and you don't want to stay at the top of a tree in a high wind any longer than you can help. I remember I was in that very predicament when the idea first came to me. If you have to pack eggs in a box without divisions, the only safe way is to *roll up* each one in a strip of cotton-wool; otherwise you are very likely to find when you get home that they have all collected into one corner, and it is sure to be the best that is broken.

Stick.—The next necessity is a stick. Of course everyone knows the value of a hooked stick in climbing a tree, but if you take my advice you will borrow that when you need it, and for your own use carry a long light hazel or something of the sort. The thick end will help you along the road, and the thin end does for poking about among nettles, beating bushes, etc., and will find you lots of nests that are just out of reach of the ordinary walking stick. It should be long and thin, but *stiff*, so that if you can get hold of one that was cut last year it will serve the purpose better than a green one.

Mirror.—Another very useful thing is a small mirror, like those periscopes made to fix on the point of a bayonet, which you can rig up to go on the end of your stick, so that you can see into nests up above in a hedge or tree without climbing right to them. Not only is it a prickly business at times, but you may make the bird desert, or leave traces which will give away the nest to the next comer; so that it is worth while to make sure that a nest has eggs before you disturb it.

Scoop.—The next thing you need is a small wire scoop for getting eggs out of holes. This is easily made, the scoop part out of the finest wire you can get, and the shank of stouter iron wire, thick enough to stay in any shape into which you may bend it. It need not be much more than a foot long, as you can easily bend it on to a stick if you want to reach further. It takes up no room in your pocket when folded up, and you should never go out without it.

Field-glass and Camera.—A good field-glass is very useful indeed, and if you have a camera that will focus down to 3 feet or so, you will naturally take that along, too.

Note-book.—You may think a note-book is nothing but a nuisance, but believe me if you come across a bird or a nest that you don't know, you will do far better to write down anything you notice about it *on the spot* than to trust to your memory. If you only notice that the bird has a speckled throat, or a bar on the wing, or something of that sort, the index at the end of the book will give you a pretty good idea what it is.

§ 2. WHERE TO LOOK.

Roads.—Roadsides are not such good hunting grounds as they used to be, owing to the amount of dust that motor cars raise; but the lanes and by-roads are still fairly free from this nuisance, and wherever you are going to a good part of your walk is likely to be on the hard road. Your long stick is very useful for beating hedges and banks and the near sides of ditches, and you save a lot of time by its use, as without it you would be looking into all sorts of holes, most of which would turn out to be false alarms. If there are four of you going along a road, it is best for two to take the sides of the road, and the other two the further sides of the hedges, so as to miss nothing. If you are alone it will generally be better to hunt the sunny side, unless the other has very much better cover.

Any kind of hedge is worth looking at, but especially the small, well-clipped sort, and the very tall. Steep banks, old walls with crevices in them, beds of nettles, and bramble-bushes are all useful places along a roadside; and ivy-covered walls nearly always produce something, though ivy on trees is not quite so good. The only way to hunt a dry ditch is to walk right along it. You not only see both sides of the ditch, but get nearer to the hedge beyond.

Woods.—Big woods look tempting, but small ones are generally better for nesting. If you see Jays or Magpies about a small wood you can find their nests quickly enough, but you may spend a long day in a big wood and have very little to show for it. Then the smaller birds are hardly to be found except round the edges of the big wood, while a small one with undergrowth may have nests in any part and at any level. A good plan with a small wood is to go up to every nest early in the season and throw down all old Woodpigeons' and Squirrels' nests, leaving the Magpies' and Carrion Crows' and Sparrow-hawks' on the chance of a Kestrel or an Owl taking them on (unless they are very ancient, or the trees very hard to climb).

Perhaps the best wood of all is a long strip with a burn running through or beside it. As to trees, fir woods give better results up aloft as a rule, while oak, beech, etc., show a greater number of small birds on the ground floor. So if your strip has some of each, you've got the ideal wood for birds nesting.

Water.—Ponds are always worth visiting, and marshes likewise; there may not be a great variety of birds, but there may be some rare ones. And you can get as wet as you like, perhaps wetter.

Running water seems to attract any number of birds, and there is no better plan for a birdnesting ramble, long or short, than to follow the course of a stream. It seems to lead straight from one good place to another, and such a walk will introduce you to more different birds in the time than any other I know of.

Open Country.—In going across country, besides ponds, marshes, small woods, good hedges and thickets, which I have mentioned already, the things best worth turning aside for are quarries, especially disused, old limekilns, ruins, outlying cow-byres, rough corners of fields, and single bushes. Of course any stretch of heather or bent grass has its own particular set of birds, and a bracken-covert may hold a Woodcock early in the season, a Greyhen in the middle, or a Nightjar at the end. Whins, too, are very favourite nesting places, and you can tackle them better when they lie in scattered clumps than when they are all in a thick solid mass. If you come across a young fir plantation, with the trees about shoulder-high, and plenty of rough grass below, you are sure to find something in it, especially round the edges.

Dwelling-Houses.—Finally, although some birds have to be sought right out in the wilds, it is always worth while to make a careful search, if possible, in gardens, farm-buildings, etc., as this list of birds that have been found nesting in the grounds of Corchester will show. And there are few places where they have to put up with so much noise and disturbance:—

Thrush.	Robin.
Missel Thrush.	Chaffinch.
Hedge Sparrow.	House Sparrow.
Greenfinch.	Yellowhammer.
Redpoll.	Garden Warbler.
Whitethroat.	Starling.
Willow Wren.	Swallow.
Wren.	Skylark.
House Martin.	Great-tit.
Blue-tit.	Spotted Flycatcher.
Coal-tit.	Wheatear.
Pied Wagtail.	Partridge.
Pheasant.	Lesser Whitethroat.
Goldcrest.	Woodpigeon.
Blackbird.	

§ 3. WHEN TO LOOK.

Time of Year.—It is most important to know the time of year when different birds are to be expected to lay, especially the rarer kinds for which one makes special expeditions; and the best way to make sure of this is to study the calendar at the end of the book, which will give you a good idea of the order in which to look for them, though the dates may be a good deal later than those I have given, which are " records."

Another useful piece of knowledge is, which birds are likely to have second broods, and that I have always given in my account of the birds themselves. You will often not be able to find a nest till the young ones are hatched, but the second nest will generally be somewhere near the first, if not in the very same place. Soon after the young have flown you should see the old birds building again, and a little patience will generally put you on the right track.

The calendar is a good rough guide, but you must watch the weather as well. For instance, if we have very wintry weather in March, the early birds may easily be a fortnight or more behind their time; but it does not follow that the summer birds, which mostly get here about the middle of April, or later, will be put back in proportion. If the weather turns warm and everything begins to grow, the later birds may be well up to time. Another year the cold snap may come after the early birds have got well started, and then it is the summer birds that will be late in arriving and behindhand with their nesting arrangements.

Birds will generally not start building until the particular cover they like has grown up enough to give them shelter, but you will often come across impatient spirits that won't wait for this. I have even seen that shy bird the Corncrake busily building its nest when the grass had not grown tall enough to hide it.

Time of Day.—So much for the time of year. Now for the time of day. I think boys would agree that all day long is the best time, but most of us have other things to do, even in the holidays; while at school the time for birds nesting is generally when you can, not when you like. Still it will be useful to know what the birds are doing at different times, and the first thing to think about is that all birds are early risers, and get the best part of their day's work over before we start ours. Now the most interesting way to study them is to watch the whole business from building (or even pairing) to hatching and fledging, and if you want to see them building, early morning is the time. They work harder then, and seem less suspicious of human beings.

Mid-day.—When the eggs are laid and the birds have begun to sit, you may find the nests of most of them at any time of the day. But there are certain birds which are very shy, and always seem to get off their nests long before you come near; then they sit about and watch you, and won't go back to their nests however patiently you wait. You can spot every pair of Whinchats in the district, but you will have hard work to find a single nest before they start to feed their young ones.

Dusk.—Now the best way to find their nests is to mark the spot where you always see the birds, and come back at dusk. Walk quietly over all the likely ground, poking about with your stick, and if you are lucky the bird won't leave her nest till you actually touch the tuft that covers it. This plan will serve for any birds that build on the ground and leave their nests in a hurry. I have walked right up to a Curlew on a *misty* evening, and walked round her at about five yards distance, and all she did was to twist her head round till I thought she would dislocate her neck; I went on and left her still sitting on her eggs. Not very like a Curlew at ordinary times, was it?

Rain.—A real wet day gives you a splendid chance for getting on terms with the shy birds, as no bird likes to leave her eggs to get wet; so you can't do better than spend such a day on birds that have always beaten you before, perhaps a Curlew, Redshank, or Golden Plover. But wherever you go you can rely on every bird being on her nest.

Snow is even better. I was once walking over a Yorkshire moor in April, seeing lots of birds about, but not coming on many nests. Suddenly a heavy snow shower came on, and I sat down under a wall for shelter. That shower didn't last for ten minutes, but before it was over I saw five Plovers, a Curlew and a Redshank come back to their nests on the piece of moor I could see, and also saw a Carrion Crow hurry into a little plantation in the distance. I found all their nests, and several more from which the birds rose as I topped a small rise on my way to the plantation; so you see how a little bad weather can help. Of course, with a *covering* of snow you can find every Plover's nest for miles. You can see the brown patches among the white 40 yards away.

§ 4. HOW TO LOOK.

Eyes and Ears.—You will never make much of a birds-nester if you do nothing but search for nests. Get to know the birds, both by sight and by sound, and you will have far more success and get far more fun out of it. If you hear a Jay screech once, or catch a glimpse of him sneaking into a wood in the early morning, you will think it worth while to climb up to every nest in the wood till you find the right one. Whereas if you went in just hunting for nests in general, by the time you had been up to a dozen or so of old Squirrels or Woodpigeons, and got your eyes and mouth full of dust, hands and knees and face scratched, and twigs and pine needles all down your back, you would most likely get fed up with the whole thing; but not half so fed up as that morning a month or so later, when you found the whole wood full of young Jays, screeching in every tree, and realized what you had missed. I remember being in a wood one morning with some boys, and hearing a Garden Warbler singing at the opposite edge. We walked straight to the sound, and presently arrived at a bed of nettles and brambles which ran all down the side of the wood. At the first poke of the stick out flew Mrs. Garden Warbler off her nest, and we had our reward. Of course, if we had spent half an hour beating out that bed of nettles we should most likely have found that nest and perhaps one or two more; but that particular morning we had to get home to breakfast, and in any case I think you will agree that our way was far the best.

I have tried in this book to tell you as much as I can about the look of the birds, and sometimes about their notes as well, but the last is very difficult. You will generally find if you *whisper* such words as " Whee-you," or " Quick-be-quick," you will get a good idea of the call they are meant for, but a great many of them can't be put into words at all; anyhow I advise you to do all you can to get to know every bird you fall in with.

HOW TO LOOK.

Some birds one seldom sees, but their voices are generally to be heard near their nesting-place. Others are easily recognized either by bright colours or striking attitudes, or peculiar flight. Nobody who has ever seen a Kestrel or Kingfisher in flight, for instance, will have much difficulty in knowing them next time. And the more birds you know, the more likely you are to spot the rare ones when you come across them. If you can get a good look at a stranger close to or through a glass, you should be able to find his portrait in a bird-book when you get home; or if you look up his points in the index at the end of this book you may find out all about him even quicker.

Now suppose you know what bird it is, but nothing else, this book will tell you whether it is time for eggs yet, and if so where to look and what sort of nest to expect. And that brings us to the actual searching for nests.

Experience.—Nobody is very good at finding nests until he has found so many that he *generally* knows exactly what he is looking for. Any hole in a bank looks like a Robin's nest at first, but once you have learnt his particular trick of packing in the dead leaves you won't waste nearly so much time on mouse-holes. And your first Plover's nest is generally a bit of a shock; you feel as if you had been staring hard at those eggs without seeing them—as you probably have; but each one you find makes the next easier to see, because you are getting to know *what to expect*. So experience will teach you far more than any book, but I will try to give you a few hints that may be helpful.

Hedges.—Hedges and bushes are often very thick, but you can see through most of them by getting underneath and looking upwards. The hedge round a wood may be closely clipped on the outside, but get into the wood and you will have a good view of any nests that are in it; and these hedges are often very good.

Woods.—Go very quietly among the trees. When you see a likely-looking nest, one should go and tap the trunk of the tree, while the other stands back where he has a good view, not only of the nest you are after, but of the trees round about, for your tapping may easily put other birds off their nests, and it saves time and trouble if you can see exactly where they come from. You should not abandon a really promising nest if nothing comes off, for a Sparrow-hawk often sits very close, and Owls generally do so, while I have even known a Magpie to wait till I was half-way up the tree before she would move.

When you *are* up a tree, even if the nest is empty you can often see into various others in the neighbouring trees, so that it may easily be worth while going higher while you are about it.

Squirrels' Nests.—You should get to know a Squirrel's nest when you see it from the ground, if possible, and you will save yourself some trouble. It may be in any part of the tree, from the trunk to the end of a branch. It is seldom round, more often the shape of a Rugger football, but flattened at the top and bottom. The nest is cased in twigs, which generally have their thin ends pointing all one way, and are not woven round and round as a bird builds; inside is a mass of fine grass, moss, etc., with a hole burrowed in at the side; but this stuff is just packed in and no more *built* than a mouse's nest or a hedgehog's. If you find one lined with soft down (the squirrel's own), you may expect to find young ones in it shortly. I have generally found them about April 1st, but sometimes later in the Summer.

Squirrels build both Summer and Winter nests (the latter generally low down and against the trunk), and as they get more solid with age they last nearly for ever, so that the woods get full of them, and they are an awful nuisance. Throw the old ones down and they won't trouble you again. I have known a brown owl to use one for her nest, scratching through the top to make a place for her eggs, but they are not worth leaving on the chance of that, as she would rather have a Magpie's nest anyway.

Undergrowth.—The best way to explore nettles, brambles and other thick cover is to poke about *quietly* with your stick, so as not to disturb the small birds till you are nearly touching them. If you make too much noise they will slip away unseen and unheard; and you will frighten pheasants off their nests, when if you parted the stuff gently you could generally have a good look at them and leave them undisturbed. This is best for all parties, as nothing will bring a keeper along so surely as hearing a pheasant get off her nest in a hurry.

Open Country.—If you are looking for Curlews and other birds that rise at the sight of man, you should take advantage of hollows and walls and anything that will hide you, so as to appear suddenly and unexpectedly on the scene. Then if you see a bird fly away *low*, and in a big hurry, go straight to the spot, and its ten to one you find a nest. A bird rising a long way off is hard to mark, but if two of you can manage to appear at the same moment about fifty yards apart, and each mark the *line* of the place and go straight for it, the nest should not be far from where you meet.

Birds with covered nests mostly sit close, and the best way to find them is to walk in line, two or three yards apart, up and down the likely places till you have covered all the ground.

Holes.—You should have a look at all holes, whether in trees, walls or rocks, as the supply is limited and lots of birds want them. Often you can see right into a hole, and a match or a flashlight will help with the darker ones; but even when the hole is too deep to see into, there are generally some signs to show if it is occupied, such as odd strands of hair or moss sticking about the entrance, or a sort of dirty polish round the edges, made by the bird rubbing against the stone or wood as she goes in and out. Of course a spider's web across the hole will show you that it is *not* occupied, and if there are no signs you still have your little wire scoop to settle the question one way or the other. A little hook will soon bring up something to show if there is a nest there.

Ponds and Lakes.—Often the weeds are so tall and thick that you can't see where the nests are. If there is a decent tree anywhere near, shin up it and you will see all you want; but don't forget to mark the spot on the bank from which to start for each one, while you are up there, for they will be just as invisible as ever when you are on the ground again. There is a certain lake where I have done good work with field-glasses from a crag alongside, even to counting the eggs in the nests; but there it was very important to mark your starting-place right, as you had quite a long walk round to get there.

Wading.—Remember a pond is generally soft at the bottom and deeper than it looks, and if you find you have to turn your trousers further up before you are half-way there, come right back and take them off—circumstances permitting. Of course if the owner is likely to come down like a wolf on the fold . . . . but we all have *some* common sense! There is not much danger in ponds, and you can soon tell if it is getting too soft for you. If there is a hard bottom under the mud you can go in up to your chin.

Swimming.—You may have to swim for some nests. It is worth it for sometimes like a Great Crested Grebe, or sometimes there is an island in a lake that is worth visiting. But *don't* try it at all unless you are a really good swimmer and sure of yourself anywhere; and if you are, beware of the weeds that don't quite reach the top of the water. If you do get into a patch by mistake, keep your legs up and you'll get through all right, but if you let them down you may easily get tied up. When you get to tall reeds or bulrushes you can pull yourself along by them all right with a few scratches, even if you can't get a footing among the roots, which is rather a risky thing to try, as if you break through it will most likely take a rope to get you out. And the nearest rope?—probably too far for you.

One other point: if you go swimming, take something to bring your eggs back in. Nature has forgotten to give us any pockets, and you will need your mouth for breathing. What you take I leave to you. I *have* used a field-glass case, but it didn't improve it.

Watching.—So much for searching for nests, and very good fun it is. But there is another way of finding them which is even more exciting, and that is watching the birds till you get them to show you where the nest is. It needs plenty of time and patience, and boys are apt to be short of both; but once you try it I think you will get more satisfaction out of one nest found this way than a good many you have come upon haphazard. You not only have the joy of beating the birds at their own game of patience, but you get to know them and all their little ways, and there are few sights more fascinating than a wild creature going about its business with no idea that you are watching it.

I don't suppose you will care to spend much time watching any but rare birds, or birds whose nests you can't find otherwise; but often you will want to sit down for a rest, or lunch, and if you choose a likely spot, where you are fairly well hidden but have a good view, you will often find birds betraying their nests before you have been there ten minutes. I was once sitting with my back against a tree (watching some Pied Flycatchers in the distance) when a Willow Wren flew down and into her nest less than one yard from my left foot. I had not been there ten minutes, but I *sat perfectly still*, and that is the whole secret of watching birds, or any wild creatures.

Now for some practical hints. We will suppose you have disturbed the birds, but failed to find the nest. Choose a spot, not too near, from which you have a good view of the place where the nest ought to be. If you can get well hidden, so much the better; but remember the nest may be quite a long way from where you think it is, so make sure of your *view* first and foremost. If you can't hide yourself and see as well, choose a good background, hedge, tree-trunk, wall or bank, and a *comfortable* seat; for once you have settled down, you must not move till you have won the game (or lost your patience). And don't be in a hurry to think you have got the secret; birds are sometimes very cunning. I was once watching a Wheatear which I knew must have a nest in a loose stone wall. The first time she went into a hole

I was delighted, but just as I was going to move, out she came again, and in the next twenty minutes she was in and out of twenty different holes. When at last she seemed to have gone in for good I could hardly believe it, and gave her five minutes by my watch before I went and looked; but it really was the nest this time.

There is one dodge which will shorten the time you have to wait, if you can manage it. Take a friend with you as far as your hiding-place, and when you are settled down let him go right away about his own business. The birds will watch him safely off the premises, forget all about you, and carry on as if they had the whole place to themselves. They seem to have no head for mathematics, and think $2-1=0$. Perhaps two or more assistants going away would work better, but I have never tried it.

You will find field-glasses most useful at this game, when for any reason you can't get near the spot, as well as for finding out what sort of bird you have seen at any time, without going so near as to frighten it. If you see a bird with building material in her mouth *before* she sees you (as you very often will with glasses) you ought not to have long to wait before you have her secret. Then it is best to mark the spot carefully, but *not* to go near it till you have given her time to lay her eggs. Many birds are very touchy at such times, and will leave a half-finished nest if you so much as look at it.

When the birds are sitting, you may be able to steal up unobserved within sight of their haunt, when it should be easy to find the nest if you can see *both* birds; but if only one is on view the other is most likely on the nest, and you had better waste no more time, but walk boldly about the place till you either find the nest or see the other bird about. Then you can retire to a respectful distance and start on your game of patience.

FIG. 3—CHAFFINCH

(see page 63)

Fig. 4—Linnet

(see page 65)

You have to be very keen to play this game in the wet; but don't forget that there is nothing like rain for bringing birds back to their nests in a hurry, and you can often be taking shelter from a heavy shower and doing a bit of detective work at the same time.

§ 5. CLIMBING.

Trees.—Tree-climbing is not dangerous, and does not tax your nerve like rock-climbing, so that with practice any boy can become a respectable climber; but you should not try a really high tree in a strong wind. If you do you will soon find out why.

Before you start to climb a difficult tree, have a good look at it and choose the best way to get up. Then as you go up take notice of how you get round the awkward corners, or you may get stuck on the way down. I have more than once had to rescue people from that predicament.

Branches are of two kinds, live and rotten (all dead branches count as rotten); and while almost any live branch, however small, will bear your weight if you put your foot right where it joins the trunk, you should never trust the other sort. The best way to do with them is to get a good hold with both hands above, and kick them hard. If they break off there is no fear of your using them on the way down (when you can't always see where your feet are going), and if they stand kicking they are pretty sound, though not to be trusted with your whole weight. In fact wherever you are you should always have one good hand-hold in case anything gives way; and up amongst the top branches keep one arm round the main one, especially when you are transferring eggs from nest to box.

In a rookery the branches are never too thin to bear your weight, or a man's for that matter, for the Rooks know just as much about rotten branches as we do, and more. So you never need be afraid to go to any Rook's nest, if your head will stand it; but the straighter up the branch goes, the better, as if your foot slips you don't slip out into space.

Swarming up a bare trunk uses muscles that don't often come into play, but anyone can do it with practice. The first Sparrow-hawk's nest I ever found was in a Scots fir with no branches for about 30 feet, and thicker than any I had tackled before; but the bark was good, and I managed to get up 10 feet or so before I had to give in. I wanted that nest, so I tried the next day and the next, in fact I probably had seven or eight goes at the tree, and each time I got a foot or two higher, until at last I managed to reach the first branch, and the nest. Even then there were no eggs in it, and several more visits were needed before I got my egg; but I never had much trouble in shinning up after that first time.

Probably the most annoying tree to climb is a tall larch, beloved of Magpies, covered with little dead branches, none of which will bear you, and all of which have to be broken off as you go up. You begin by breaking off as many as you can reach with your stick, and then climb as far as you can, stripping the tree as you go. Next you slide down again (slowly) and lie on your back awhile, surveying your handiwork. When you feel better, up you go again and break off some more. This time you ought to reach the first sound branch, but if you feel you are losing the grip with your legs, come down and repeat. I once grasped that first sound branch just as my knees refused to grip any longer, and it wasn't so sound as it looked. I never came down a tree quicker, and with all those little broken stumps it wasn't only my trousers that were torn to ribbons.

I once got to a Magpie's nest in a tree like that by climbing a tall thin spruce that was conveniently near and getting a good swing on till I was able to catch hold of the other tree and step across. This trick is not hard, but needs some judgment in letting go of the first tree. That reminds one of a Carrion Crow's nest in a pollard willow down in the Fens. The tree was very old and hollow all the way up, but round the crown were branches as big as young trees. Most of these came out at the side and turned straight up, and would not have borne a man for a minute, and the nest was in one of them; so although there was a nice soft river to fall on I felt like giving it up, till I spotted one slim branch that grew straight up from its base and stood well above the nest. I went up that one and persuaded it to bend the right way till I could get my hand into the nest. So you see there are sometimes other ways of getting to a nest than the first that strikes you.

I have said nothing about climbing irons because I don't think much of them. I may have been unfortunate in those I have tried, but *they* certainly were much better for telegraph poles than for trees with bark on, not to mention a nasty wound in the leg I gave myself with one of them. Also I don't think they are very safe on a really big tree, and you should be able to manage a moderate one without them.

Rocks and Ruins.—Rocks and ruins are a very different proposition from trees, and a fair number of grown-up men break their necks every year rock-climbing. So my advice to boys is "let them alone." But birds build their nests in them, and where the nests are boys are sure to go, so I had better give a few hints on how to take care of yourselves.

First of all study the climb before you start, just as you do with a difficult tree; then when you have started, come back again rather than go round a corner or across a gap if there is *any* doubt about getting back the way you came. And for goodness sake don't be too *proud* to turn back; you'll get lots of chances of showing your pluck without risking your neck. You will often find things very different up there from what they looked like from below.

If you are climbing down from the top, which I hope you won't do often, turn your face to the cliff; and beware of a *slope* that gets steeper as you go down.

Never go up a *crumbling* cliff higher than you care to fall; and don't trust a stone embedded in earth so that you can't see its real shape. And above all things don't have anyone climbing above you, or climb above anyone else; that is the very worst thing you can do. I was nearer death once in a quarry in the Cotswolds than I ever was in the Great War, through a friend up above sending down a big piece of rock—and all for a few Jackdaws' eggs!

Ruins are not so treacherous as rocks, and it is easier to judge distances from below by the size of the stones, but they make very nasty climbing for all that. You generally have only fingers and toes to support you, and on a perpendicular face it's a case of one slip and down you go, with generally a heap of loose stones to land on. So let them alone if you can, and if you can't, be cautious.

There is just one time when you may try fancy tricks on a cliff or wall-face; and that is when you are certain to fall into deep water, always supposing you can swim, of course.

Have nothing to do with ropes, unless you are with a *man* who really understands the business.

§ 6. WHAT NOT TO DO.

" Don't " is a word schoolboys hear far too much of, but it has figured in all good advice since the Ten Commandments, and you must forgive me for using it rather freely here. I am going to tell you your duty towards the birds, the farmer, the keeper, and yourself.

Birds.—Your duty towards the birds is to upset them as little as possible. Most of them are afraid of you to start with, but try not to make matters any worse. Therefore—

Don't take more than one egg as a rule. No collection wants two eggs of the same type, though you may have a score of different Blackbirds' eggs, say, and still have hopes of a new variety. But when the bird only lays two eggs, leave them if she has begun to sit, and take them both if they are fresh; for then she will soon lay again, and it is hardly fair to make her spend all her time on bringing up a single chick. And how dull it must be for the young one!

Of course if you found the famous clutch of 18 Blue-tits' eggs in a small hole it would be your *duty* to take about half of them, and save that family from the horrors of the Black Hole of Calcutta, for most of them would be smothered for certain.

Don't take an egg that is nearly hatched, for you will never get it blown decently. You can tell if most light-coloured eggs are fresh, by simply holding them up to the light, when you can see the yolk shining through; but the unfailing test is to put the egg into water. A fresh egg lies flat at the bottom, but as hatching goes on an air-bubble forms at the broad end, which gets bigger and bigger as the chick develops; and in a few days the egg will stand on its point at the bottom, then it rises to the top, and the longer it has been sat upon the more of it shows above the water. If it only floats like a sponge, just touching the surface, you can blow it easily. In marshy ground, or even in a damp ditch, you can often get enough water to test an egg by simply digging your heel well in, when the hole you have made will soon fill. If the one you try is very far gone, you may as well test them all. If there is an addled egg it may float, but will not bob up like the others.

Don't think that a nest is deserted simply because the eggs in it are cold. They always *are* cold until the bird has laid her full number. If she started to sit before, the young ones would all hatch on different days, which would never do.

Don't disturb a nest more than is absolutely necessary or you may make the bird desert. And when you go to a nest try to make no tracks, or at least hide them as much as possible before you leave, and see that the nest is as well covered up as it can be; for the next person who comes along may *not* know his duty towards the birds, and anyhow you don't want to *help* him to find your nests.

Always remember that the birds are giving you no end of a lot of fun, and it is only playing the game to help them when you get the chance, and at least to do as little harm as you possibly can.

"DON'T." 23

The Farmer.—Your duty towards the farmer is to give him as little annoyance as possible (and he is easily annoyed).

Don't let him see you on his land. If you are any good at scouting you should generally be able to manage this; and even if he is a friend you don't want him to think you are *never off* his land, or he will soon begin to think you a nuisance.

Don't disturb his sheep at lambing time.

Don't leave his gates open and let the stock out into the high road or into the young crops.

Don't break down his fences. It is just as easy to test the strength of a rail before you put your weight on it as it is to make sure of a branch at the top of a tree. If you should bring one down, try and fix it up again, and always put back any stones you may knock down in climbing a wall. And remember that the best place to climb a gate is as near the hinges as possible.

Don't walk through standing corn or hay; there is always room for one at a time along the hedge side.

There is a big difference between simple trespassing, for which you can be turned off a man's land, and trespassing and doing damage, for which you can be prosecuted.

The Keeper.—Your duty towards the game keeper is to be friends if you can; but it will generally be more than you can manage to make even a neutral of him. He is much more likely to class all boys as "vermin," and act accordingly.

If it is peace, he is the man to tell you how to know the signs of the woods and the ways of the wild things in them; and what he says about the bigger birds is generally true, though he is not always very learned in the smaller ones.

If it is war, you must keep out of his way as much as you can, and take care that if you do meet him he has as little as possible to grumble at.

First of all, don't let him catch you on his beat. This means more scouting, and rather more difficult. Of course if you see him crossing the fields on his way home to tea you know where you have him for an hour or so, and that is the time for any special place you want to visit. But you will not often know where he is, and if you don't want him to know where *you* are, the most important thing is to make no noise, whether with your voice or your movements, or by setting a whole lot of Woodpigeons crashing out of the trees. Then if you stick to the hedges in going across country you will be hidden on one side, and much less conspicuous on the other, than if you boldly parade across the middle of the fields. In a wood you can often hide better by standing quite still under a tree than by making a dash for better cover. A keeper is not unlike the wild creatures he watches in some ways, and any *movement* is sure to catch his eye, for that is what he is chiefly on the look-out for.

Secondly, don't disturb game birds on their nests. You may make them desert, and they will certainly make a tremendous racket, which is what you want to avoid. And don't take their eggs, for what is just an egg to you now, may mean a sporting shot and a good meal for someone next autumn. If you want specimens of their eggs, you have only to visit a few nests just after hatching time and you are sure to find an addled egg or two, which are just as good when blown, even if the inside does smell a little high.

Finally, don't leave any traces that you can help, or meddle with traps or other appliances, or you are more than likely to get a warm reception when you go again.

Once more simple trespass is one thing and trespass in pursuit of game another which may get you into several different kinds of trouble, from heavy fines to hard labour.

Yourself.—Your duty towards yourself is something like this. Don't let well-meaning but ignorant people give you eggs, and don't above all things buy them from the " naturalists' " shops—if you do you are encouraging wholesale robbery of your friends the birds, for that is how *they* get their eggs. (There is no harm in buying a few fancy specimens of Gillemots, etc., from the professional " climmers " who get eggs for the market, and it's much better than breaking your neck.) Otherwise don't have an egg in your collection unless you have found, or at any rate *seen* the nest yourself. Every egg in your collection should remind you of the nest it came from, the bird that laid it, the search for it, the finding of it, and all sorts of pleasant things. Eggs that don't remind you of anything at all are not a *collection*; you might just as well have Seebohm's book with the beautiful coloured plates, or an album of stamps given you by your big brother when he got tired of it. Quite nice things to have, both of them, but not to be compared with a collection of eggs that you have found for yourself.

Don't be in too much of a hurry to get all the eggs there are. The season may be short, but there are plenty more coming, and it is good to have something to look forward to. The finest thing in the whole business is finding a new nest that you haven't found before, and the harder it is to find, and the longer you have to wait for it, the greater the pleasure when it does come. So don't be too ready to let kind people show you nests, and do everything except climb the tree for you (I have known them even do that); for you never get the same fun out of it as when you do it all yourself.

One more don't, and that is, don't take on trust everything you read in this book or any other. It's probably true, but the oldest of us has not done learning about birds yet, and there's no harm and lots of good in seeing for yourself. *Your* long-tailed tit may have a different way of getting into her nest from mine, and in any case it's a sight worth seeing. Again the way nests are built and what they are made of are things you should be careful to notice; and anything you have found out for yourself is always better than what you get from a book. So take this book as meant to give you an idea of what to look out for, and not as the last word on the subject.

§ 7. THE EGG COLLECTION.

Suppose you have taken all my advice, found lots of eggs and brought them home safely. The next thing is to blow them, and a little more advice will perhaps save you some breakages and disappointments. When you start to blow an egg, hold it by the *ends* between your finger and thumb, for it is stronger that way, and do the whole business over water, so that if you drop it there's no harm done. Get a good drill, and use it on eggs that don't matter much till you are pretty sure of yourself. Bore the hole where the egg will naturally balance on it, and opposite to any markings that you particularly want to show. Don't try to blow eggs with too small a hole,

THE EGG COLLECTION.

and don't shove the point of the blowpipe right inside. If you keep it just *outside*, the air goes in just as well and the contents come out much better, and you will never burst the egg. Having emptied the egg, squirt in some water, shake it up and blow it out again; and keep on doing this till it comes out as clean as it went in. Wipe the outside *lightly* with a wet handkerchief, just to remove the dirt but none of the markings, and put it hole-downwards on a piece of blotting-paper to drain. If a yellow stain appears, or the egg tries to stick to the paper, wash it out again.

Now your egg will keep for ever (?), and if you keep a note-book, you can number each nest as you enter it, and put the same number on the egg, just beside the hole; so that you can look it up at any time and find out where it came from, and all about it.

There are two good ways of keeping your eggs. One is to lay them on cotton-wool in a box or cabinet, and the great point about this is that you can easily rearrange them as new ones are added, and keep them in their proper families. The other way is to stick each egg on a card with its number in the corner; the cards can be mounted in cases or drawers, stuck on with paper hinges such as you use for stamps, only bigger, and the cases covered with glass. Your eggs are quite safe once you have got them in, you can see them very well and their numbers too, and they look very neat. In fact there is no better way of *showing* eggs. The drawback is that when you add to your collection, unless you have left a lot of spaces (and you can never tell just how many specimens of any bird's eggs you will have) you probably have to unship the whole lot to get them in their places, and it is very easy to break a few in taking them off.

If your eggs are quite clean inside and kept where the light cannot get at them, most of them will keep their colour as long as you like to keep *them*.

§ 8. THE NOTE-BOOK.

Every naturalist should keep a note-book for two good reasons. The first is that your memory plays funny tricks, and lets all sorts of useful things slip; and even brings facts out at times quite different from when they went in. If you have ever heard fishermen talking about the good old days of their youth you will know what I mean. Now, experience is the thing to help you on with your hobby more than anything; and you lose a good deal of it and get rather hazy about a good deal more, unless you have the facts to look up, just as you wrote them down at the time. You can't possibly remember such things as the dates when you found this bird or that, and the longer you go on the more useful such knowledge becomes.

The second reason is the pleasure you get from looking up old notes, which remind you of all sorts of joys you would otherwise have forgotten, patience rewarded, unexpected bits of luck, narrow escapes, and good times generally. Even the bad days are sometimes good to remember after a year or two.

We will suppose you *are* going to keep a note-book. The next question is what you are going to put in it. I advise you to put in every nest from which you take an egg, the first nest of each bird each year, any late ones or second broods, and any other that has anything specially interesting about it.

Your notes are easier to look up if you have them in columns, and a good arrangement is—

Date. No. Bird. Eggs. Place. Nest. Remarks.

I should take two pages, and give the whole righthand page to the " Remarks " column. Here you put the interesting things, such as how you found the nest, how the birds behaved and what happened later, when the eggs hatched, and the young ones flew, in fact, anything. The " Nest " column should be the next biggest, for putting where it was built, what it was made of, and anything else of interest. " Eggs " should be given as fresh, sitting, hard sat, young, and so on; and the number of the entry is most useful, if you number your eggs, as you can turn up No. 6 or No. 293 in a moment, just by the size of the number.

You don't need to put in your register *only* nests that have eggs; if you find an uncommon bird with young ones, or even see the family after they have left the nest, the date and place will give you a good idea as to when and where to look for it next year. Many birds, even when they have spent the winter in Africa, will come back to the same little corner of England, and build within a yard or two of their last year's nest; and if it is in a hole, it is very likely to be in the same hole next year.

In the case of rare birds, any record of their having bred or tried to breed in your neighbourhood is useful. For instance, suppose there is only one Chiff-chaff anywhere near you, and you hear him singing in the same tree all through the nesting season, but never manage to find the nest; if you note down the place, you will not forget to look him up next summer, and perhaps with more success.

PART II.

THE BIRDS, THEIR NESTS AND EGGS, AND THEIR BREEDING HABITS.

INTRODUCTORY.

This book was originally meant for North-Country boys, so you will find that the North-Country birds have got the biggest share in it; and I have given the North-Country nesting-times, which are always later than the South. But I have not left out the other birds altogether, and I think you will find here all you want to know about any ordinary South-Country bird. I have given a few North-Country names, where it seemed to me they might be useful, and if you hear of a "Feather-poke" or a "Smoky" all you have to do is look it up in the index, and that will put you on to the right bird.

I have not given you coloured pictures of the eggs, which are seldom much good, often lead to eggs being named wrong, and make a book much more expensive; but there are a number of photograph reproductions which should help you. I have tried to tell you first how to know the birds, then where to look for their nests, and what sort of a nest to expect, and how to tell their eggs from others that are like them. I have also told you when to look for them, and given any special habits of the bird and hints as to finding the nest where I could.

The bird is the main thing, and a book with good pictures of *them* will be useful; but even without that I think if you look up a stranger's points in the colour-index at the end of this book, you will generally manage to find out who he is.

MIGRATION.

In most books on birds you will find them called "Summer Migrants," "Winter Migrants," or "Resident Species," or something like that, and I think it may save you some misunderstanding if I try to explain a little about the migration of birds.

Every kind of bird has a certain belt of country in which it lives, because the climate suits it, and further North or South would be too cold or too hot. But within that belt the birds are free to move about as they like, and *nearly* every bird goes South for the Winter and North again for the Summer. The result is that the Northern part of their range is deserted in Winter, and the southern in Summer; and as they can't be moving about and nesting at the same time, every bird has reached its own " farthest North " by nesting-time. So you see most birds migrate both in Spring and Autumn, and the only difference between the three kinds I mentioned is that the country we live in happens to be at the North end or the South end of their range, or in the middle of it.

So when England is about the northern limit of a bird's travels, that bird nests with us and is not to be found in the Winter, and people call it a Summer Migrant; and if it is at the Southern end we only see *this* bird in Winter and call him a Winter Migrant, for we live in the strip of his territory that is deserted when the birds go North in Spring. Fieldfares and Redwings are Winter birds with us, but no doubt people in Norway call them Summer Migrants, for that is where they go to nest.

The so-called Residents you can see all the year round, and as all Thrushes or Blackbirds are very much alike, you are apt to think that the birds themselves are fixtures; but keep your eyes open in the Spring and you will see lots of signs that they are changing their quarters, too, even the Thrushes in your own garden. Take a walk about the middle of February, and make a note of all the birds you see (it will not be hard work); then make the same round a month or six weeks later and you will be kept busy counting them, and there will be a lot like Pied Wagtails, Greenfinches, and many others that weren't on your first list at all. And all this before the " Summer Migrants " have begun to come in.

Again, if you live in a smoky district where all the birds get pretty grubby, you will see them apparently putting on new feathers in Spring, and suddenly appearing clean and bright. Now birds moult in Autumn, and though they do get brighter in Spring, it is more often by the faded edges of the feathers wearing off than by a change of feathers; and in either case it can't be done in a single night. So those beautiful bright Yellowhammers sitting about the hedges this morning were not the grubby ones you saw yesterday, but a new lot from some cleaner countryside further South, come to take their places.

Often you will see our breeding birds paired and settled down in their nesting haunts, while there are still flocks of the same kind of bird in the places where they have been all Winter. These are going further North, where it is colder, and they have the sense not to go so soon as *our* birds, which have come from France or Spain perhaps.

If you should come across a Pied Blackbird, or any bird that is easy to recognize, you can soon tell whether he goes away for the Winter or not, especially if he turns up next Summer and nests in practically the same place,

Fig. 5—Yellowhammer

(*see page* 68)

Fig. 6—Reed Bunting

(*see page* 70)

MIGRATION. 33

as one used to do in our garden. But you can't tell how far he has gone, as you are hardly likely to meet him in your travels. It is very hard to tell how far some birds go, but I can give you some idea of the long-distance travellers. Willow Wrens get as far as Shetland in Summer, and there are none to be found this side of the Mediterranean in Winter, so they must go a matter of 2,000 miles or so, and so do most of the Warblers, the Swallows, and I think most marvellous of all, the Corncrake. And there is at least one bird that nests in the Arctic circle, and doesn't have any Winter at all; for he crosses the equator and has another Summer in South Africa. That is the Curlew-sandpiper, and I believe some others do the same.

So you see the easiest way to get to know about Migration is to try and spot the birds that don't migrate at all, for there are very few of them. Partridges and most game birds you can be sure of; the Dartford Warbler, Nuthatch, Heron and Dipper all seem pretty stationary; but you can study that question for yourselves if you like, by keeping a lookout for birds during the Winter.

If I were to go on telling you all I know, or think I know, about the migration of birds, I should be robbing you of the pleasure of finding things out for yourselves, and I might never get this book finished. But it is a most mysterious and fascinating part of a bird's life, and I hope the little I have told you will encourage you to keep your eyes open for signs of it.

I suppose every one notices the first Swallow and the first Cuckoo, but there are lots of interesting events in the bird world which you may observe long before the first nest is found or the first of the " Summer " birds appears; and if you note them down in a sort of

"Visitors' book," and compare one year with another, you will find this record becomes almost as interesting as your nesting notes.

ARRANGEMENT.

Now I am really coming to the birds, but I must just say a little about the order in which I have put them. It is quite easy to put them in their right families as a rule, but you can hardly find two books in which the families are arranged the same way, and so I have made up an order of my own which may not be very scientific, but is easy to understand.

I have gone by their feet, and have taken the tree birds first, then the ground birds, and lastly the water birds.

The tree birds include all the perching birds, like Thrushes and Finches (and everyone knows what their feet are like), the Pigeons, which are really very different but manage to perch too, the climbing birds, with two toes in front and two behind like the Woodpeckers, and the birds of prey. Among the perchers you will find the Dipper which is a water bird, and the Skylark which prefers the ground, but look at their feet and you will see they are both perching birds which have taken to other habits.

The ground birds are the game-birds, rails and waders. You will find the Coot and the Waterhen have taken to the water, but belong to the rail family all the same.

The water birds begin with the Stork tribe (the Heron) followed by the Pelicans (Cormorants), then come the Duck tribe, the Gull tribe, and the Auks Divers and Grebes.

Now we come to the Perchers, and the first four families are those that *walk* when they are on the ground.

FAMILY I.—THE CROWS.

The birds of prey used to head the list in the old books, but the Crows have taken their place now that they have been found to be the most highly-developed of the birds. You can tell that by their cleverness, and I am afraid by their wickedness, too, for they are all thoroughly bad characters, and not one of them but is a thief at least. They all have big strong beaks, black feathers as a rule, and hoarse voices, all in keeping with their characters. They are afraid of nothing but a gun, and except the Jay, they don't bother much about hiding their nests, but choose high trees and steep cliffs, where they build their castles like the robber barons of the bad old days. The Magpie even goes in for fortification, and no other bird has much chance of getting at her nest when she is at home. Their eggs are mostly of a dirty greenish colour. They generally take less than three weeks to hatch, and the young ones come out naked, blind, and helpless. They are easy to tame if you get them before they are full-feathered, and make good pets because they are so clever; but they are all thieves.

I.—THE CARRION CROW (OR " CORBIE ").

Bird.—This is a solitary sort of bird, and you will not often see more than two together except round a dead sheep or some delicacy of that sort. That ought to prevent you from mixing him up with the Rook; but there is also a difference which you can see at very close quarters, or with a glass. The Corbie has feathers right down on to his beak, whilst the Rook has a bare whitish scaly patch of skin round the beak, reaching back to the eyes. His cry is a deep sort of croak which you will soon learn to distinguish from the cawing of Rooks.

Haunts.—The nest is generally to be found in a small wood, and the further away from man the better. The favourite tree is a tall Scotch fir, if it can be got; but they will use other trees, and nest in rocks where there are none.

Nest.—It is built of sticks and lined chiefly with wool, and generally neater and better finished than a Rook's, but otherwise much the same.

The birds come back to the same spot year after year, and even when the keeper shoots them both, others will come just the same, as if they had a sort of register of "building-sites to let." They sometimes use the old nest again, but more often build a new one close by.

An old Corbie's nest is a great favourite with other birds, as you will see from the history of one in Stanley Wood near Corbridge. In May, 1903, the Crow hatched off her brood, and from the look of the nest I was pretty sure it had been used before. In 1905 a Kestrel brought up four young ones in the same nest, a Sparrow-Hawk had it in 1907, and a Horned Owl in 1908; and for all I know there may have been others. In 1909 the nest was a bit flat but still holding together, so there is no doubt about the Corbie being a first-rate builder.

Habits.—The bird is very wary and slips off before you get near as a rule, so if you want to find out which of four or five is the new nest the best way is to steal up to the spot at dusk or on a wet day, when you ought to see her get off the right one.

Eggs.—The eggs are generally five, mottled with various shades of green and brown, one of them often much lighter than the rest. I think this is the last laid, but you may be able to find out for certain. Most of them you can't distinguish from Rooks' eggs, but there is a very dark green type which is fairly common, and which I have never seen amongst hundreds of Rooks'.

Young.—The young ones astonished me the first time I saw any, with their pink skins; I was so sure they must be black.

Season.—The eggs are not laid much before the middle of April.

More Habits.—The old Corbie is a thief and a murderer, and plays havoc with the eggs and young of game, and of the larger birds generally. You will often find traces of his work, especially near water, to which he takes his spoils to wash the sticky egg off his beak, or because raw egg makes him thirsty. (I don't *think* he tries them in water to see if they are fresh, for I don't believe he minds that, though he's quite clever enough to do so if it mattered to him.) I have sometimes picked up quite respectable specimens at such places, and the hole is generally in the right place though rather big. A Greyhen's egg I found like that was the first hint I had that they bred in the district.

He is one of the few birds you should treat as an enemy; for he does a lot of harm and no good, and can hardly be called ornamental. But if you rob him he goes somewhere else and starts again, so as a rule it is better to leave some eggs and let the keeper have a chance at him.

2.—THE ROOK.

Habits.—Everybody knows the Rook, and it is not hard to find a Rookery. The birds come back to their old nests year after year, and one of the first signs of spring is when they visit their old homes, which they very often do early in the year; this seems to be just to have a look round and see what repairs are needed, as they go off again for some weeks before they begin to patch them up in earnest.

Trees.—It is easy enough to find the rookery, but not so easy to get the eggs, for they always choose the tops of the highest trees; but most rookeries contain a few trees that can be climbed. I knew a rookery in a clump of tall beeches that became so populous that some of the birds took to building in a small fir plantation alongside. This was a godsend to bad climbers, but you must not expect to get a chance like that more than once in a lifetime. If you want Rooks' eggs you will have to climb for them.

Nest.—A Rook's nest is always untidy, partly because it has to be patched up, or perhaps rebuilt on the ruins of the old one, and partly because of overcrowding. The birds can't choose the fork that will just suit them when every branch has to bear two or three nests, so they must build wherever they can get two or three twigs to stick. The nest is strongly built to stand the gales, sticks outside, mud next, and inside a variety of lining stuff which you will see for yourself when you get there.

Eggs.—Five eggs is the usual number, and their dirty greenish and brownish markings are laid on in all sorts of ways, so that you may collect any number of different sorts, and still not be without hopes of finding a new one. As far as I know you don't find special types in each rookery, but that is a thing you can study for yourselves.

Season.—There should be eggs before the end of March, and bad weather doesn't put them back much.

Rook-Shooting.—The young ones are regularly shot in May, when they leave the nests; for though Rooks have their uses, they do a lot of damage at certain times, and must be kept within bounds.

3.—THE JACKDAW.

Bird.—You can tell the Jackdaw among a flock of Rooks by his smaller size and rather quicker wing-beats in flying. Near at hand you can see a grey patch covering his cheeks and the back of his head, and nearer still his light blue eyes. His croak is very short and sharp, sounding rather like his own name "Je-ack," and generally given only once at a time.

Haunts.—Jackdaws nest in colonies, like Rooks, but always in holes, either in cliffs or ruins or hollow trees; but any kind of hole will do at a pinch, so don't be surprised to find them in chimneys, or in rabbit-holes in a sand-cliff. You will often find great numbers nesting together, and very seldom a single nest all by itself.

Nest.—The nest is big or little according to the size of the hole, always untidy, and made of sticks and various kinds of rubbish, with a shallow cup for the eggs lined with almost anything soft. I have seen the greater part of a "Yorkshire Post" built into a Jackdaw's nest. Sometimes they have to put up with a great cleft in the rocks that a man could stand up in; then they pile in sticks till they have filled it nearly to the top, and make their nursery right at the back of the little space left. Some of these nests would nearly fill a cart.

Jackdaws are famous for carrying off all sorts of bright things to their nests, but I have had no luck in the way of finding silver spoons, etc., in them; perhaps you may.

Eggs.—The eggs are generally five, but sometimes six, and are cleaner-looking than most of the family's, being very pale blue with scattered spots of various colours, some of them nearly black; and the shell is very smooth and polished.

Season.—They don't lay much before the end of April. I have found them very late, and they *may* rear two broods sometimes, but none of the other Crows do.

Habits.—Jackdaws are egg-thieves like the rest, and do a lot of damage among Gulls' nests or others that are easy to find, but they don't seem to be much good at finding hidden nests.

4.—THE MAGPIE (OR " PYOT ").

Bird.—You can spot a Magpie a long way off by his black-and-white plumage, long tail and peculiar dipping flight; and early morning is the time to see him out in the open, and find out where he is building his nest. His note is a peculiar chatter, both loud and long, very like the noise you can make by rattling a handful of shot in a tin; and he doesn't mind making himself heard if he is excited.

Haunts and Habits.—Magpies nest in various places, but their main ideas seem to be to get high up, and keep well away from the next pair. Where they are scarce they build chiefly in woods, one nest to a wood; but if there are plenty you will see the great big nests in belts of tall trees, single trees, high thorn hedges, and even in bushes six feet high, out on the moors where trees are lacking. There is nearly always a nest near a marsh of any size, which is a fine place for egg-hunting; for that is the Pyot's hobby, or rather trade. The keeper knows this, and where keepers are plentiful, Magpies are rare.

Nest.—If there are plenty of trees, they generally choose a tall larch, and begin to build before the end of March. First a big deep cup is made, of sticks well plastered together and lined with lots of mud. Next comes a dome of thorny sticks which covers in the whole nest, except for an entrance at one side. That finishes the outside, but inside it is far too big, and has to be lined out and filled up; and for this they use nothing but roots. The sides are attended to first, and soon it is narrow enough but still about 18 inches deep, and it has to be filled up to about four or five inches before it is ready for the eggs. The whole thing is often three feet from top to bottom, and I used to find my magpies' nests from the train, going home for the Easter holidays.

I have never found anything but roots in the lining, and it is easy for the birds to get them where there are ploughed fields; but up among the hills it must be very hard to get the quantities they need, so if you ever find nests in such places you should look carefully and see if they have used anything else instead.

These nests are great favourites with the birds that do not build their own, and are worth visiting on the chance of finding an Owl or Kestrel.

Eggs.—The eggs are often as many as eight or even nine. They are pale blue, thickly freckled with greenish-brown and grey, and vary a good deal, but not so that you could mistake them for any other birds' eggs And the nest is like nothing else on earth.

Season.—The nest takes so long to finish that you will seldom find eggs in it before the middle of April, and often not till May.

When you find a nest building, note exactly how far it is finished, and you will soon get a good idea of when to go for eggs to any nest you may find.

5.—THE JAY (Fig. 1).

Bird.—This is a very shy bird at nesting-time, and the earlier you are up the more likely you are to get a sight of him. He flies as a Magpie would if his tail were shorter, and if he is going away you can see the white patch on his rump, just above the tail; if you get a good look at him his crest and brilliant blue wing-patches will leave no doubt as to who he is. His cry is the most discordant even in this family, and when he lets out one of his screeches there is no mistaking it; it is rather like what you hear when someone sits down heavily on the cat, but louder.

In summer, however, he does not show off his fine feathers or his powerful voice often, and you may pass his nesting haunt every day and know nothing about it; so you need to know him well and use your eyes and ears if you don't want to miss him altogether.

Haunts.—His haunts are woods, big and little, and where there are plenty of them and not too many keepers he is not uncommon—for he is on the vermin list like the rest of them, for egg-stealing. For nesting he likes thick cover, leafy underwood when he can get it, and there you will find the nest at the top of a slender ash, elder, or holly, perhaps, where the leaves are thickest, or up a big tree in one of those bunches of twigs that sometimes sprout out from the trunk. Up North he is more likely to be in a fir-wood, and the top of a young tree is the place for him there; though I have known Jays to nest regularly in a wood of tall larches, which of course only grow leaves at the top, and here every nest was 40 or 50 feet up, and still visible from the ground. If you suspect a Jay's nest in any wood, always look for it where the cover is thickest.

Nest.—The nest is made of twigs outside and roots inside, neat and compact, just like a Magpie's without the roof, but smaller of course, with a shallower cup and no stiffening of mud.

Eggs.—The eggs are from five to seven, much the same colour as a Magpie's but smaller, and the spots smaller too. They vary, and some might be taken for a Blackbird's, but the nest will always tell you which they are.

Season.—You will not find the eggs before the middle of May, and perhaps even later in green woods where the nest has to be hidden by leaves.

When the young ones are fledged, the vow of silence is broken, and you hear the whole family screeching one against the other.

Note.—The Jay is the only one of the family that goes in for hiding his nest, and before he has beaten you as often as he has me, I expect you will admit that he is pretty good at it.

OTHER MEMBERS OF THE FAMILY.
6.—THE RAVEN (Fig. 2).

The biggest of the lot, all black, with a way of soaring like an Eagle, and a very deep croak. You can tell him from a Corbie by his *rounded* tail. A few pairs nest in the crags in the wildest parts of Northumberland, and in most of the mountainous parts of England. The eggs are not much bigger than a Corbie's and are sometimes laid before the end of February, so if you should get the chance of visiting a nest, don't go too late.

7.—THE HOODED CROW.

Also called "Grey Crow" or just "Hoodie." He has a grey back and breast, but is otherwise just like a Corbie in his habits, nests, eggs and season. He takes the Corbie's place further North, and you may find him anywhere in Scotland, but he only comes to England in the winter. The West Coast is where he is commonest, and he often nests in cliffs. Some used to breed in the Isle of Man, and perhaps do still.

8.—THE CHOUGH.

Or "Cornish Daw" has a red beak and legs, and is all black elsewhere. His habits, nest and eggs are like a Jackdaw's, but he is rare and getting rarer. He nests in the cliffs at various places on the coast from Cornwall to the Isle of Man.

FAMILY II.—THE STARLINGS.

Only one of these breeds in England, but he makes up for that by being very common. His walk reminds you of the Crows, and so does his general build, and his cleverness; for you can tame him and teach him to talk or whistle tunes. He imitates other birds perfectly, and I have often looked round for a Curlew in the distance when it was only a Starling whistling on a chimney-pot. I once taught one to whistle a tune, by giving him a lesson from my window every morning as I was getting up. He used to sit and sing just outside, and whenever he stopped I would strike up; he soon picked up five or six bars, though there were one or two notes he never got quite right.

Bird.—He looks black in the distance, but get him really close to, in the sunshine, and you will see that he has some wonderful colours on him. His notes are many and various, and I need not try to tell you about them.

Haunts.—Starlings like to nest in holes, whether in trees, rocks or buildings; but they are so common that there are not enough holes to go round, and they have to put up with what they can get, so that you find them building in spouts, ivy, and all sorts of queer places. If they can get in under the tiles of a roof they will build there, and it is a common thing to hear them scuffling about above the ceiling, or to find them flopping down chimneys and issuing forth into a room, covered with soot and very excited. Where there are Green Woodpeckers the Starlings nearly always seize upon their holes, so the Woodpecker has to spoil a new tree every year; and I have known rare birds like Pied Flycatchers to turn up in Spring, wanting to nest in a wood, and have to move on because the Starlings had got every available hole.

Nest.—The nest is a loose arrangement of straw, lined with feathers, and its size depends on where it is built; under the tiles there is not room for much, but when a Starling sets to work to block up a water-spout it is quite the other way on.

Eggs.—Five or six eggs are laid, pale blue or sometimes pure white, without any markings. It is a common thing to find odd ones lying about on lawns or short grass. Most birds are absent-minded like this at times, but Starlings especially so.

Season.—April is the time for the first brood (though I have known eggs to be laid as early as February), and as soon as the young birds leave the nest the old ones start away with a second lot in the same hole.

Young.—Young Starlings make a great row in the nest, and if they are causing annoyance about the house you can take them out of the nest and put them in the garden (in some sort of cage to stop the cats getting them). The old birds are sure to find them, and will come and feed them just the same.

The young ones are grey all over, and when they are out you will find flocks of them about the hedges for a day or two. After that I don't know what becomes of them, but you may perhaps find out if you keep your eyes open.

FAMILY III.—THE LARKS.

These are not much like the Starlings, but I put them next because they *walk* on the ground instead of hopping.

You know they sing on the wing, and have a way of fluttering their wings that makes them seem to have two pairs. What you don't see until you have one in your hand is the very long claws they have on their hind toe. If you find any young ones you should look and see if they are born with this, and if not, when it begins to grow.

Only two larks breed here, and one is very rare.

I.—THE SKYLARK (OR "LAVEROCK").

Bird.—The most noticeable thing about a Skylark when he is not flying is a sort of crest on the top of his head. You know his flight and his song, and have most likely noticed how fond he is of dusting himself in the road on fine days.

Haunts.—The lark nests on the ground, in grass fields, stubbles, or even plough, and not uncommonly on the grassy edges of a road, where you may find eggs and nest covered with dust. Up on the moors he prefers white ground to heather, and nests among tussocks of bent, if there is any.

Nest.—The nest is made of grass entirely, and lined with the finer kinds. I have never noticed any hair, but it may be used. It is well hidden among the grass as a rule, and the bird always walks to and from it, often making a little run or track which you can see if you have sharp eyes. Now and then you may find one quite bare, and then the hole is rather deep and narrow, not like the covered sort.

Eggs.—The eggs are from three to five, and rather large; whitish in ground colour, and mottled pretty well all over with olive brown. Sometimes no white can be seen, often most of the colour is in a ring round the thick end, and I have seen eggs where the colour was laid on quite evenly all over, but these are very rare.

Habits.—The Lark is a good mother and sticks to her nest through thick and thin. I remember one which built in our cricket field and laid two eggs. As the grass had to be cut next day we destroyed the nest, thinking she would make a new one in the next field and finish her job in peace. But by the next evening she had established herself in a hole where a cricket ball had been squashed into the ground by the roller; and there she laid her other two eggs, and sat on them when there was no cricket going on. We hoped she would hatch them, but in a week or so she gave it up.

Season.—April or early May is the Lark's laying time, with a second brood in July; but I once found young ones full grown on April 13th, so it may sometimes be worth while to look for them in March.

Hints.—If you see pairs getting up together, they have not begun to sit yet, but when single birds keep rising you may begin to hunt for nests. Towards evening is the best time to find them at home, and two of you can cover a lot of ground by dragging a rope between you across the pastures. The birds will not often leave their nests till the rope touches them.

2.—THE WOODLARK.

Very rare, even in the South, and hardly ever seen in Scotland. Yet there are some that spend the Winter in England, so they don't migrate much.

It is a smaller bird than the Skylark, and has no crest, and shows no white in its tail. Its song is not so cheery, but has sweeter notes in it. It settles on trees between its singing flights, and rises from the ground in circles, not straight up like a Skylark. It sometimes haunts the edges of woods, but more often open spaces with trees.

The nest is like a Skylark's and the eggs similar, but smaller and marked with reddish, not greenish-brown. You might confuse them with the Tree Pipit's but these are smaller still. Once you get to know a Tree Pipit's song, you should spot the rarer bird if you are lucky enough to hear one, and you will not take one for the other. Another point is that the Tree Pipit is a summer bird and doesn't have eggs till late in May, while the Woodlark starts early and has two broods like the Skylark. And if you heard one singing in March . . . .?

Fig. 7—Robin

(see page 77)

FIG. 8 WILLOW WREN
(see page 85)

FAMILY IV.—THE WAGTAILS AND PIPITS.

These are the last of the perching birds that walk. They all have the two outer pairs of tail-feathers white, except the Rock Pipit, which has them grey. They all wag their tails, but you don't notice it so much in the Pipits, their tails being much shorter. They have various chirping calls, but the Tree Pipit is the only one that can be called a singer. They are insect-feeders, and a Cuckoo often pops an egg into one of their nests. Nests and eggs are not much alike, nor the places where they build, but they are all good sitters. The young ones hatch in about a fortnight. The Pipits come first because they are very like the Larks.

I.—THE TREE PIPIT.

Bird.—This is a speckled brown bird, rather like a Lark, and often wrongly called "Wood Lark," or sometimes "Bank Lark," and you will know him best by his singing. He sits on the top of a tree from which he rises every now and then singing a short song which reminds you rather of a Lark's. At the end he dives down head-first on to his perch, giving four or five clear whistles as he comes, like "whoo-ee," "whoo-ee," etc., and by these whistles you may know him a long way off.

Haunts.—He is a Summer bird and arrives in April. His haunts are open woods with grass under the trees, parks, and fields with trees in them, roadsides and waste places such as quarries and clay-pits; there must always be a tree for *him*, and generally a bank for *her*.

Nest.—The nest is nearly always in a bank of some sort, though sometimes in a tuft of grass on the level, under the trees. It is very well hidden, but the cock will tell you where to look, and the hen generally stays on till your stick nearly touches her. She is a plucky bird, and I have seen her skip into the road, spread out her wings and tail, and try to frighten me away from the nest.

The nest is well built as a rule, chiefly of grass and perhaps a little moss, with a few dark horsehairs in the lining.

Eggs.—The eggs are from four to six, and I know three different types. The first is like a Lark's, but the colour red-brown; the second, nearly as common, is like a Reed Bunting's with rich purple spots and short streaks, on a light ground also purplish; the third, very rare, is olive green, laid on rather like the last; and there may be others. You will need at least a dozen to show all the changes.

Season.—They have only one brood, but some begin by the middle of May, others not till June.

2.—THE MEADOW PIPIT.

"Titlark," or Moss-cheeper."

Bird.—This is very much the same sort of bird as the Tree Pipit. He cheeps a great deal and doesn't sing much, but you may see him diving down on to a wall, giving the same sort of whistle as the other bird.

Haunts.—He is very common, though more so in Summer than in Winter, and is always to be found on the high ground where there is bent or heather; and he specially favours the marshy parts of the moor. His name of " Moss-cheeper " hits him off exactly.

Nest.—The nest is always on the ground, and a very favourite place is in the side of a tussock of bent. The bird sits very closely, and unless you keep your stick busy you may walk right past her. It is a neat little nest, nearly all of fine grass, and often lined with nothing else.

Eggs.—Four eggs or sometimes five are laid, looking very dark in the nest; but when blown they go lighter, and have a greyish tint in the brown, which prevents you from mistaking them for the reddish kind of Tree Pipits. You are much more likely to take them for Skylarks', but of course they are too small for that.

Season.—You may find their eggs any time from April to June, but whether the later nests are second broods I cannot say. There is no time when you can say that the first broods are out and the second not begun, as you can with Starlings or Chaffinches.

Hint.—Don't forget that you may always hope for a Cuckoo's egg in a Meadow Pipit's nest after the end of May.

3.—THE ROCK PIPIT (OR "SEA MOUSE").

Bird.—Much like the other two, but darker, and with grey feathers in the tail instead of white.

Haunts and Nest.—It only nests near the sea, but is fairly common where there are rocks. The nest is nearly always on a ledge of rock, or steep bank, hardly ever on the level ground. It is well tucked away in a crevice of the rock, or hidden among the grass or seaside plants, and is built in much the same way as the other Pipits'. The bird sits well, too.

Eggs.—The eggs are a *little* bigger than either, not red-brown or grey-brown, but just *brown*, though they vary a good deal. If you notice the bird's tail as she flies off there will be no doubt about it.

Season.—The eggs are laid early in May, and there is often a second brood.

4.—THE PIED WAGTAIL.

This is the commonest Wagtail, and well known to everybody, as you can tell by the number of names it has, such as "Nanny Washtail," and so on. You very seldom see one in the North in Winter, but by the middle of March they are all over the place—we are very near the edge of its Winter range.

Haunts.—As a rule you are wise to look for Wagtails near water, but this one may be found nesting in walls, quarries, or limekilns where there is none at all, probably because it is so common; for in years when they are scarce, you often find the dry places deserted, but very seldom those near water.

Nesting Places.—The nest is built in a hole or crevice of some sort, nearly always one with a wide entrance. I have found them in stone walls of all sorts, bridges, limekilns, old buildings, stacks of bricks or drainpipes, cliffs, quarries, heaps of big stones; occasionally in ivy on a wall or bank (in holes in pollard willows in the South), once on the bare ground under a big stone, and once in a bundle of peasticks. I hope you will find some in stranger places still.

Nest.—It is an untidy affair made of coarse stalks of plants and various rubbish outside, but well lined with wool and hair (nearly always *grey*, and I think certain birds generally choose certain colours, but you can look into that question for yourselves if you like). The cup is right at the back of the nest as a rule, and the front sloped out well forward, evidently to make the whole thing look like a heap of rubbish that has just drifted in —and so it does to anyone who doesn't know just what to look out for.

Eggs.—About six eggs are laid, pale grey with light brown spots, and rather shiny. The colour is always the same, but the markings may be many or few, and a good collection should show about six varieties, not counting freaks. They vary enough to tell you pretty well if it is the same birds that come back to the same places each year. Some Sparrows' eggs are just like Pied Wagtails', but you can't mix them up (except in your collection if they are not marked).

Young.—The young ones have short tails, which is just as well when you think of six of them in one nest; but they soon grow after they begin to fly about.

Season.—The first lot of eggs is laid at the very end of April, the second in June.

5.—THE WHITE WAGTAIL.

This is the Continental form of the Pied Wagtail, and only a few ever come to England, and hardly ever to the North. It differs from the other in having the back *grey* instead of black. Eggs, nest, and habits are all much the same, and unless you know your Pied Wagtail well you may easily miss the rarer one. Many hen Pied Wagtails have grey backs (and so have young birds), but if you see the pair of them, and *both* have grey backs, you can be quite sure they are White Wagtails.

6.—THE GREY WAGTAIL.

Bird.—You would naturally call him the Yellow Wagtail, for that is what he looks like with his bright yellow breast; but you can easily tell him from the true Yellow Wagtail by his slate-grey back, the cock bird's black throat, and the fact that he has the longest tail in the family, and the Yellow the shortest.

Haunts.—You are more likely to see odd Grey Wagtails about in Winter, but in summer you meet about one for every six Pied Wagtails. But you know just where to find them, for they must have not only water, but running water, and not only that, but rocks beside it; and if you show me the rocks and running water I'll show you a Grey Wagtail—most times.

Nest.—The nest is always near the water side, and the favourite place is a sheltered crevice or corner in the rocks, though you may find it in some hollow in the bank, often under a projecting stone.

It is made of roots and moss, and lined chiefly with hair. Very often it is three-cornered, fitted in the angle of rock like a corner-cupboard, the front sloping back and looking like a clump of moss, while the cup for the eggs is right back in the corner—the same idea as the Pied Wagtail's, but worked in different materials. Of course this is only when it is built in a corner.

Eggs.—The eggs are five as a rule, freckled all over with pale brown, with generally a black streak or two on the larger end; and they don't vary much. Two other wagtails lay the same sort of eggs, and so does the Sedge Warbler, but none of them build in the same sort of place.

Season.—The breeding birds often turn up a week after the Pied Wagtails, but they get to work quicker, and you may find their eggs a week sooner, or even in the second week of April. They always go in for a second brood, though they often only lay an egg or two and leave them.

7.—THE YELLOW WAGTAIL.

Bird.—This is the stumpiest of the wagtails, not so graceful as the last bird, though he is very dainty-looking; all yellow below and olive-green above, with a yellow streak over the eye. No contrasts in his colours, and no black throat.

Haunts.—They are Summer birds in England, coming about mid-April as a rule, and are getting very few by the time they reach Northumberland, most of them stopping further South or going up to the West side of the country.

They are found in marshy fields by the riverside, or on open commons, or by a lake. They go a good way up the dales, but not right up the hill burns as Grey Wagtails do.

Nest.—They always build on the ground, in a bank or tuft of grass, or even under a clod of earth in a cornfield, and the nest is well hidden; but though the place is just what a Pipit would choose, the nest is the proper wagtail kind, of various materials, and with a soft felted lining.

Eggs.—From four to six, and just like the Grey Wagtail's.

Season.—May for the first brood, and, I believe, there is generally a second.

8.—THE BLUE-HEADED WAGTAIL.

This is the Continental form of the Yellow, with the same short tail, and the only differences are—

The head is blue-grey.

The streak over the eye is white.

The back is greyish rather than greenish.

This is the rarest of the lot, and the only reason I give it is that almost the only place in England where it has been found nesting is near Gateshead, and what has happened once may happen again.

If you find one (its nesting habits are the same as our Yellow Wagtail's) keep it dark till the young ones disappear—*then* you can write to the papers and say what county you found it in, no more.

That brings us to the end of the perching birds that *walk*. I am coming to those that *hop* next, and we have a lot of them. First the Finches, a big family which includes the Buntings. Next the Thrushes, a much bigger family, which includes the Warblers and some other birds besides the true Thrushes; and finally the Dipper and the Wren, which have each a family to itself.

FAMILY V.—THE FINCHES.

You will know a Finch best by his broad strong bill, which is meant for cracking hard seeds; and the whole lot feed on seeds of one kind or another. As a rule then they are not very useful to man, and those that eat grain quite the opposite. We used to reckon them fair game for the catapult or air-gun in Winter, but let the insect-feeders alone.

They are all small birds, from the Hawfinch which is a good deal less than a Thrush, to the Redpoll, no bigger than a Bluetit. You can generally tell the cock birds from the hens by their brighter colours, and some of them are very handsome. A few of them sing very well, and they nearly all try to.

Their nests are generally in bushes or trees, but a few prefer the ground—and everyone knows where a Sparrow likes to build. Their ways of building are many and various, and so are their eggs, though you can see the family features in most of them. They all hatch in about a fortnight, and the young ones come out naked, blind, and helpless, like most of the perchers.

I.—THE CROSSBILL.

You must have seen his portrait, and noticed how the two halves of his beak cross over one another, so I need not tell you what he looks like. He is a rare bird, and you may never see one all your life. On the other hand you *might* find half-a-dozen nests next March, and this is the reason. They keep together in parties all the year round, and travel about the fir woods, living on the cones. (That's why they have a beak like a pair of wire-cutters.) They don't much mind where they go so long as there are plenty of cones, and when February comes round they settle down to breed wherever they are—and next year it may be in that big wood near you.

You may see the birds (the old cocks mostly red, and the old hens mostly yellow, and the rest anything from brown to green), or you may hear them cracking the cones, which is more likely in a thick wood. Then if it is March, or even the end of February, look about for nests.

Nest.—They will be fairly close together, generally in Scotch firs, high up or low down, in a fork or on a flat branch. Both nest and eggs are very like a Greenfinch's, but the bird sits very tight, and will let you have a good look at her, and you are probably two months ahead of the Greenfinch's nesting time, so there can't be much difficulty.

Season.—They have only one brood, and often begin to lay before March, when very few people are about the woods, so they may often be missed altogether, and not be so rare after all.

2.—THE HAWFINCH.

This is another rare bird, but you might get one with luck, as it seems to be getting less rare each year.

Bird.—It is bigger than most of the Finches, with a big head and very stout beak, quite enough to recognize it by, *if* you see it. But Hawfinches in the nesting season are as shy as Jays, so that is not likely. At a distance they look very like big Chaffinches, with whitish wing-bars and a good deal of white in the tail. The cock bird sings in a fashion, but there aren't very many people who could recognize his song for you, and his call-note, something like " sit, sit, sit, sit," is not loud, and won't catch your ear.

So you see you are more likely to find this nest by chance the first time, but if you do you should hang around till you know all the bird's notes thoroughly, and are sure to spot them the next time you hear them.

Nesting Places.—The nest may be found almost anywhere where the cover is good, in a fir or an evergreen, or in ivy on a tree trunk, and either high up or low down, but never *very* low. And though woods are this bird's favourite haunts, nests have been found in all sorts of places, such as gardens, orchards, and even high hedges.

Nest.—It is a big flat nest, mostly made of thin twigs, with a well-finished cup in the middle lined with moss, fine roots, or hair.

Eggs.—The eggs are often as many as six, a size larger than a Sparrow's, generally pale green with dark streaky markings. The streaks and the big nest will leave no doubt as to what you have found.

Season.—The middle of May is the time you may expect them, but they are often later.

3.—THE BULLFINCH.

Bird.—You will know a Bullfinch as it flies away by the white patch above its tail. The cock bird is very handsome, with black head, red breast and a white bar on the wing; the hen the same but duller everywhere (except that white patch). The beak is very broad, even for a Finch.

Once you get among their haunts you will soon get to know the little call-note they give as they flit about, and you *may* hear the cock-bird singing, but he is very quiet about it.

They are quite rare, and you may have to wait several seasons before you find a nest. You can't rely on them coming back to the same spot to breed, and they may suddenly appear where there hasn't been a nest for years.

Haunts.—Woods are their haunts, and a favourite place for the nest is on a flat branch of a fir tree, not very high, though often above your head; but other places are often used, and you may find them in any kind of bushy place or a thick hedge. I know a hazel-covert for instance, where they breed fairly regularly.

Nest.—The nest is rather flat, made of thin twigs, with a cup in the centre made of roots and hair, or sometimes all hair.

Eggs.—The four or five eggs are *blue*, with dark brown spots and streaks, often making a ring round the thick end, and you cannot mistake them for any other Finch's eggs. The nest is peculiar too, and the bird generally sits closely enough for you to see her before she goes.

Season.—They begin to lay about the middle of May and generally have a second brood.

4.—THE HOUSE SPARROW.

There is not much to say about this bird, except that he is far too common and does endless damage.

Nest.—The nest is built in a hole when one can be got, but many birds have to do without and build in trees. You may even see them among the sticks of Rook's nests, and everyone knows how they throng in ivy on a house. The nest they make in a hole is just a mass of straw and feathers and anything that comes handy; but they can build a good nest when they like, and if you go up to one in a tree or high hedge, you will find a great dome of straw with a hole at the side, quite weather-proof and very comfortably lined with feathers.

Eggs.—They lay five or six eggs, and the varieties are endless. You never can be certain your collection is complete, and it is always worth while looking into their nests on the chance of finding some new freak. And another thing—unless you mark your eggs you will be mistaking your Sparrow for anything from a Pied Wagtail to a Meadow Pipit.

Season.—Sparrows begin early, and bring out brood after brood, sometimes going on till nearly Christmas.

5.—THE TREE SPARROW.

Bird.—You know the difference between a cock Sparrow and a hen. Well, a Tree Sparrow is like a cock Sparrow (you can see the differences in their pictures best), but there is one point that is fairly easy to see; if he has *two* white bars on the wing instead of *one*, he is a Tree Sparrow. A better point still is that cock and hen and young all are alike; and if you think you have got a Tree Sparrow's nest you can always make sure by waiting until you can see both birds at it.

Haunts and Nests.—They are rare birds, and not found much near houses, more often in the woods and fields. They build in holes of all sorts, and in old nests of Crows and other birds, and the nests are just like House Sparrows', but I don't think they ever build the domed nests in trees and hedges, though, of course, that can hardly be proved. I *have* found a nest in an old Corbie's, not among the sticks but in the flattened-out cup, and it was roofed over.

Eggs.—The eggs are generally five or six, and very like the House Sparrow's though not nearly so varied. They are smaller and smoother as a rule, and there is one kind with brown markings very thick all over, which I have never been able to match with House Sparrows' eggs. But you never can be *quite* certain unless you see the birds at the nest.

Season.—They begin in April or early May and have at least two broods.

6.—THE GREENFINCH (OR " GREEN LINNET ").

Bird.—I expect you know this bird pretty well, for he is very common, and you are sure to see him in Spring sitting stolidly on top of a tree or bush. You hear him too, and I can't describe his various notes very well, but he always seems to call his wife " Mary." Just at pairing time he does show some excitement, and takes wild flights that don't seem to lead anywhere, so that he seems to have gone mad for the time being.

Haunts.—Gardens are his favourite resort, but there aren't enough of them for all the Greenfinches, so you will find plenty of them about the hedges. I remember finding seventeen nests with eggs in a lane near Cambridge that wasn't half a mile long.

Nest.—The nest is often built in an evergreen, or a high thick hedge, not seldom in ivy on a tree-trunk, and occasionally right up in a tree top; and you cannot often reach it from the ground unless all the hedges are low. The most extraordinary place I ever saw for one was in a hole in a pollard willow, two feet in and built among the rotten wood.

It is rather a flat nest, made of roots and a few twigs outside, then moss and various soft materials; and nearly always has an untidy and ragged look, though the cup is often well finished. The birds seem very fond of wool, and you don't find many nests without it.

Eggs.—From four to six eggs are laid, white with a few blotches and streaks in two shades of brown. Some of the other Finches' are like them, but the nest is a good guide, and you can generally see the bird on it, though not after she slips off; for she makes no fuss, but just disappears, and this is the way with most of the Finches.

Season.—You may find the first nests in evergreens late in April, but in the hedges it will be nearly the middle of May as a rule (as soon as the leaves are thick enough to hide them). There is always a second brood, and sometimes a third, at any rate in Yorkshire where I used to find a good many nests with eggs in August.

7.—THE CHAFFINCH (Fig. 3).

Called " Spink," " Scobbie," and "Apple-shealer."

Bird.—No need to describe him, but in case you don't know his cheery song, you can hear it any fine day in February, when few others are singing.

You can tell the cock from the hen pretty easily, and in Winter they go about in separate flocks; it is quite interesting to notice just when these flocks break up and they begin to pair. They settle down in their nesting quarters very early, and you see them long before the Yellowhammers or Greenfinches begin to turn up.

Haunts.—You will find Chaffinches everywhere, in gardens and orchards, in woods and along hedges; so their nests have to be built in all sorts of places, but the favourite is a fork, in a fruit tree or tall hawthorn.

Nest.—The nest is the neatest and most beautiful I know, and the greater part of it is made of moss mixed with spiders' webs. It is smooth and compact outside, with a deep and beautifully finished cup lined with hair, feathers, etc., and it is hard to know which to admire most, the inside or the outside. For it is shaped to look like a swelling of the branch, and the finishing touch is a trimming of little scraps of lichen fastened on with spiders' webs, to make it match the grey bark—and I rather think you will find the amount of grey varies to suit the place where it is built, though most birds go by instinct more than by common sense, and build the same sort of nest, whatever the surroundings. I found a nest once where the grey effect was got with little scraps of newspaper, and another where chips of rotten wood were used for the same purpose.

No one can see a Chaffinch's nest without wondering how it is done, and the finishing off of the inside most of all. Most of us have tried to fool someone else with a sham nest, and discovered how hard it is to make one anything like the real thing. Well I'm not going to tell you how it is done, but if you want to find out, the best way is to look out for a Chaffinch's nest beginning, in the Easter holidays, in a place where you can see it from a window, or some hiding-place; and what you see will explain the mystery, not only for the Chaffinches but for all other birds as well. And I think you will be surprised to see what a simple business it is.

Eggs.—Four or five eggs are laid, and when you have once seen their dark purple-brown spots, often with a sort of pale reddish stain spreading round them, you will never mistake them for anything else. If you should find a pale variety, very like a Greenfinch's, the nest and birds should tell you at once which it is. Chaffinches *do* make rather a fuss at their nest, perhaps because they have taken such a lot of trouble over it.

Season.—You should find eggs early in May, and a second lot about mid-June.

8.—THE GOLDFINCH (OR " GOLDSPINK ").

Bird.—The Goldfinch is very rare in the North, and I believe in most places, so if you *should* see a little bird that reminds you of a Chaffinch, but has a broad yellow bar on each wing and bright colours generally, you had better drop all your other plans and watch him.

Nest.—An orchard is the likeliest place to find the nest, but I have seen it in a scrubby sort of fox-covert, and on a common. It is like a Chaffinch's but smaller

FIG. 9—WHITETHROAT
(see page 90)

Fig. 10—Lesser Whitethroat

(*see page* 91)

and not quite so perfectly finished; and it is generally built pretty low down.

Eggs.—The four or five eggs are practically white, with markings like a Greenfinch but smaller and not so blotchy. The eggs are a good deal smaller too.

Season.—You will not find them till well on in May, but the bird often starts a second brood in July.

9.—THE SISKIN.

Nest.—This bird nests regularly in Scotland, and has been found occasionally in most parts of England, so I will just mention that it builds high up in fir-trees, and makes a very small nest of twigs, grass and roots, lined with the same sort of stuff as a Greenfinch uses.

Eggs.—The eggs are just like a Goldfinch's, and the nest might be mistaken for a Redpoll's, but *her* eggs are always a deep greenish-blue colour.

Season.—They are laid early in May, and there is a second brood.

Bird.—You will recognize the cock bird *if* you see him by his bright green colour (almost yellow) and his very forked tail. He is a good deal smaller than a Greenfinch. If you ever come across these birds, be sure to learn their notes.

10.—THE LINNET (Fig. 4).

Called " Brown Linnet " or " Lintie."

Haunts.—I have seldom found a Linnet's nest except in a whin-bush, but if whins are scarce they will use other bushes, especially young fir-trees, and sometimes even build in long heather.

Bird.—The bird is light brown with a red patch on the head, and generally a red breast too, and the rest of the under parts whitish, but you can't see much of this at a distance; and if you see a brown bird sitting on the top of a whin-bush and singing a very pretty song, he is probably a Linnet. And what is more, the nest is often quite close to his perch.

Nest.—It is generally low down in the bush, but not always; and is rough outside, often built of dead gorse twigs, but very smooth inside. Willow down is a favourite lining when it can be got, but you will find all sorts of things used in different places.

The hen bird has no red crown. She doesn't usually leave the nest till you touch the bush, and as she flies off you will see that the outer tail-feathers are edged with white.

Eggs.—The four or five eggs are smaller than a Greenfinch's, and without the bigger and darker markings as a rule. You will never take them for Greenfinches', but some small Greenfinches' might be taken for Linnets', so you have to be careful; but if you know a Greenfinch's nest well, as you should, you will know the first Linnet's for something different—and remember a Greenfinch flying off will show no white in the tail.

Season.—You don't often find Linnets' eggs much before the middle of May, but if they don't start too late they generally try to rear a second brood.

II.—THE TWITE (OR " HEATHER LINTIE ").

Bird.—The Twite has a yellow bill, no red on his head, and a long black tail, which shows a little white at the edges when it is spread. So you can tell the cock

FINCHES. 67

from a Linnet if you get a good look at him. His English name tells you what he says, "twah-it," and his Scotch name calls him what he is, a Linnet that nests in the heather.

Haunts.—He is not common, but a few *may* be found on any moor.

Eggs and Nest.—You can't tell the eggs from a Linnet's, and the nests are much alike, but a nest in the heather is not likely to be a Linnet's, and you should both see and hear the birds, which generally flit round anxiously while you are at the nest.

Season.—They only rear one brood, and begin rather later than the Linnets as a rule.

12.—THE REDPOLL.

Bird.—This is a little dark bird, with a red crown which you won't often see as she sits on her nest, for most of them are pretty high up. The cock bird is brighter-coloured, and a very fine singer indeed. You will more often hear him than see him.

Haunts.—Redpolls are rarer than Linnets, but anywhere in the North you should find three or four nests in a season. They haunt high hedges, woods, and gardens, and thickets of willows and broom are good places for them; but I would never pass a tall elder in hedge or wood without looking up among the higher forks, for that is the likeliest place of all.

Nest.—The nest is generally in a fork, and well up. It is the tiniest you will see in a long day's march, and considering that the outside is generally made of fine twigs, and the inside well lined with feathers or hair or down, it is a wonderfully neat piece of work.

Eggs.—Until you actually look inside it is hard to believe that such a little nest *can* hold six eggs, as it often does. They are blue-green, with light brown markings of the usual Linnet type, and can't be mixed up with any other kind.

Season.—The time of laying varies from well on in May to the middle of June, and I have never known of a second brood.

The Buntings.

These make a group by themselves. They are more stolid even than the other Finches, and all have a twittering sort of song. Most of them build on the ground, and use chiefly grass outside and hair inside, and their eggs are marked with long scrawly lines.

13.—THE YELLOWHAMMER (Fig. 5).

Sometimes " Yellow Bunting " in books, and often " Yellow Yowley " or " Yowling " in the North.

Bird.—There is no need to describe his yellow head and breast and his song about " A little bit of bread and *no* cheese." He has a mournful look while he is singing, and often when he is trying it over in March he leaves out the top note, the " no," as if he couldn't make up his mind to refuse the cheese, though he knows it will disagree with him.

Haunts.—The Yellowhammer is a roadside bird, and fond of his dust-bath, though it doesn't seem to dull his plumage.

Nesting-places.—The first nests are made mostly in banks or the sides of ditches, and very well hidden; but for the second nest this bird oftener chooses a thick hedge, and often builds pretty high, up to six feet at least. The cock bird sits on a telegraph wire or other high perch, singing, and gives you a good idea of where to look for the nest.

Nest.—It is made of grass and lined with hair, and the front edge is often built out into a sort of flat doorstep, which occasionally almost amounts to a carriage drive, and may show you the way into a nest which would otherwise be hidden well back in a thick hedge.

Eggs.—The Yellowhammer lays three or four eggs, pale mauve grey with dark brown streaks scribbled over them, though you may find some spotted and once in a way a plain one. Even then you can't mistake the ground colour. The cock takes his turn on them with the hen, and his yellow head has sometimes helped me to spot a nest as I walked by.

Season.—You *may* find an early one with eggs in April, but it is more likely to be the second week in May. The second nests are often still occupied at the end of July.

14.—THE CORN BUNTING.
Or Common Bunting.

Haunts.—Very rare in the Tyne valley, but generally common where there are corn-fields; and I have met him in the Yorkshire Dales right on the edge of the moor.

Bird.—He is the biggest of the Buntings, and a stout bull-necked bird with a much thicker bill than the rest of them. He has no striking colours about him, but you will easily recognize him as he sits quite still for hours on the top of a bush and utters his twittering song, like the Yellowhammer's, but quicker, and all on one note. When he flies he keeps close to the ground, and flutters his wings like a Skylark, so that you would almost think he had two pairs going.

Haunts.—Some winter in the South, but in the North they are summer birds, arriving in April and settling down in pairs about the hedgerows. You will have no difficulty in learning where there will be nests, for you can't fail to see the birds at any time of day.

Nesting-place.—Finding the nest is another matter, as it is generally in a hay or corn field, like a Corncrake's, and your best chance will be to go very early in the morning (about the middle of May) and try to see them building. The nest is almost always on the ground, under an extra big tuft of grass or clump of weeds, or a small bush—once in a way it may be *in* the bush.

Nest.—It is a proper Bunting's nest, but large and loosely made; and it may have other materials in it besides grass, roots and hair.

Eggs.—Five eggs is the average number, much the same colour as a Yellowhammer's as a rule, sometimes lighter. They are as big as a small Thrush's, and you can't mistake either them or the birds for anything else.

Season.—They wait for the grass to grow up, and you probably won't find eggs before the end of May, or even later.

15.—THE REED BUNTING (Fig. 6).

Bird.—He is also called the "Black-headed Bunting," as he has a black head and throat, but that name properly belongs to another bird. You might take him for a cock Sparrow, but only in the distance; and he sits stolidly like a Bunting, not a bit like a Sparrow, and sings like a Bunting too, often very near the nest.

Haunts.—He is not a rare bird in the spots he likes, which are always near water, and must have good cover, such as withy beds or reedy ponds in the Fens, and scrubby marshes such as you find at the heads of lakes or tarns in the North country. If you have not got such a place near you, it is worth while making an expedition to the nearest good-sized lake, as you are almost sure to find him, and have a good chance of other marsh and water-birds into the bargain.

Nest.—You will generally find the nest on the ground or very near it, among sedge, rushes, small scrubby bushes, or the stubs of a withy-bed. Poke about near where you see the cock-bird; and you ought to find it, for the hen is a very close sitter.

It is very much like other Buntings' nests, and generally has some hair in it, but willow down and reed-fluff are handy where it is built, and are often used for lining.

Eggs.—Anything from four to six is the number, and they have short thick streaks of rich purple on a lighter ground, which looks as if it had been stained with the same colour.

A Tree Pipit's eggs are sometimes very like this bird's, and her nest is similar and built on the ground. However, it is very unlikely to be built in the same sort of place, and you can't mistake the birds if you see them, as you most likely will; for they make a good deal of fuss when the nest is disturbed, and will even sham lame to lead you away from it. The hen has nearly as much white in her tail as a Tree Pipit, but her dark head and her flight will help you to recognize her.

Season.—Towards the end of May, with a second brood occasionally.

16.—THE CIRL BUNTING.

This is very much a South country bird, so I won't say much about it.

The hen you can hardly tell from a Yellowhammer, but the cock has a black throat and a black line through the eye.

It is fond of heaths and commons, and there the nest is generally in a small bush or in the heather below it. The nest is like a Yellowhammer's but the eggs have a pale blue ground and the scribblings practically black. They are laid in May, and as I have found them in July I am pretty sure there is a second brood.

FAMILY VI.

THE THRUSHES.

These are soft-billed birds and feed as a rule on insects, worms or soft fruits, so are quite different from the Finches. Only a few of them winter in England, for their food is very scarce then, and a great many go all the way to Africa. Nearly all the good singers belong to this family, in fact those that don't sing are the exceptions.

1 have to deal with twenty-three birds in this family, so I am going to divide them, and take the true Thrushes and their nearest relations in one group and the Warblers in another.

1.—THE THRUSH.

Called Song Thrush, Throstle, or Mavis, and often "Greybird," but I think this may mean a Missel Thrush as well.

Bird.—I may just say that he is smaller and browner than a Missel Thrush, and his breast is streaked rather than spotted, while a Missel Thrush's spots are half-moon shaped, and lie *across* his breast.

Food.—He is very fond of snails, and cracks their shells on a stone. Other birds do this at times, but he makes a regular practice of it; and you will often come across his favourite stone, with broken shells all round it, in the garden or by a hedge.

Very few of them spend the winter in the North, compared with the numbers that nest there, and some are quite late in coming, though not later than the end of March.

Nest.—You all know where to find them, and all about the mud-lined nest with the little chips of wood dusted over it, and you may have wondered what the wood is for. I have, and I think it must be to help it to dry and prevent the eggs sticking to it, for the Thrush doesn't waste much time either in building her nest or in laying her eggs in it. Its rather marvellous how she gets it so smooth inside, but if you have seen a Chaffinch or any other bird at work you will have a good idea of how it is done.

Eggs.—The eggs do not vary much, but some have red-brown blotches instead of black spots and I have seen them with no markings at all. Five is the usual number, and six very rare.

Season and Nesting-places.—The first arrivals begin to lay about the last week of March, generally building in evergreens or very thick hedges, or in a bank. Some start a week or two later, but very few wait for the leaves to give them cover. There are always two broods. They are quite fond of a hole in the wall, even where there are plenty of hedges, and you will find them in lots of queer places, even on the flat ground.

2.—THE MISSEL THRUSH.

Often called " The Thrush " as opposed to the " Throstle."

Bird.—He is bigger and greyer, flies with a sort of dipping motion, and chuckles as he goes. I have told you about his spots, and the only other thing is his song, which he prefers to give in a snow-storm, a habit which has earned him the name of " Storm-cock." It is quite different from the Thrush's and comes in unfinished snatches which go well with a blizzard. You should easily get to know it, as you will hear him singing often enough when no other birds think it worth while.

Haunts.—The Missel Thrush is not nearly so common as the other, but every orchard and wood and most big gardens hold a nest.

Nest.—It is often very high up, and can very seldom be reached from the ground. One of the main forks of a tree is a favourite place, especially the first from the ground; and it is not uncommon to see one right out at the end of a long branch. Another place is the top of a young fir tree, and I remember one " regrettable incident " when the tree bent so much that the eggs rolled out.

Wool.—The nest is like a Blackbird's inside, but generally has a lot of wool in the outer part, and some small twigs. I have seen one with great locks of wool streaming down a foot below, like an old man's beard.

The birds make even more noise than the common Thrushes when you find their nest, and will stand up to a Magpie or any other robber that comes along.

Eggs.—The eggs are generally four, and I have only once found five. They are hard to describe, but the markings are bold blotches of purple-brown, leaving a good deal of light ground-colour showing. You will never mistake them for Blackbirds' eggs. Sometimes one is very much bigger than the rest, and your collection will show a good many variations both in size and in colour.

Season.—The 1st of April is soon enough to look for eggs. I think second broods are the rule.

The Fieldfare.

These birds don't breed here, but as they often stay well into May, and *may* be seen in ones and twos, I will just mention that they are the same size as a Missel Thrush, but have the head and rump slate-coloured; while below they are spotted on the throat and flanks leaving the rest of the breast white, so you need never confuse the two.

Redwings are also about in Spring, but I think always in flocks. They are rather like Thrushes, but have white on the breast too, and a pale yellow streak over the eye.

3.—THE BLACKBIRD.

Bird.—Notice the big difference between cock and hen. You may have even taken the hen for a Thrush, when you just saw her mottled throat sticking out of the nest. Not all cock Blackbirds have the yellow bill, and I think they get it their second year.

You can generally tell the Blackbird's song from the Thrush's, as it has some very deep mellow notes, and not so many trills. It is more of a pipe, and less of a whistle.

I won't tell you where to look for Blackbirds' nests, as you can't help finding them; or how they are made, as you can see for yourselves.

Eggs.—Six eggs is as many as I have ever found, and that very rarely. You will need nearly 20 to show all the variations of size and colour. I have found two eggs in one nest, both pale blue, both nearly round, and one just half the size of the other. In another were five eggs, and no two of them the same size. Any nest is worth looking at on the chance of finding a freak egg.

Season.—They are a day or two behind the Thrushes, but I think they begin more together; and they start building just as soon, but have a lot to do after the mud stage, which is where a Thrush stops.

4.—THE RING OUSEL.

Or "Hill Blackbird."

Bird.—Like a Blackbird with a broad white collar crossing his breast, but not reaching right round his neck. The hen has the colours of the hen blackbird, but shows the collar all right.

The Ring-ousel has a short song, about three notes at a time, but by the tone of them you can tell he is some sort of Blackbird.

He is a summer bird, arriving about the last week of March as a rule, but many come later, and some years there are very few about, or perhaps none at all.

Haunts.—His haunts are the heather moors, and you may find a nest wherever there are Grouse. If he is there you will hear him singing any evening.

Nest.—The nest is built among the heather, generally on a steep slope; perhaps by the side of a burn, or among the crags, or in the side of one of those funnel-shaped sink-holes you may find on so many moors. It is built just like a Blackbird's. I have heard that there is no mud in it, but I never pulled one to pieces to see.

Eggs.—The eggs are just like a Blackbird's, too, though the markings are generally bigger, more like blotches than freckles; and as it is not uncommon to find *them* nesting on the moor, in just the same sort of place too, you can never be quite sure unless you see the birds. Fortunately they make just as much fuss at the nest as the rest of the Thrushes, so that should be easy. Their " chack! chack! " sounds more like a Fieldfare than a Blackbird.

Season.—The laying season depends on when the birds arrive, but generally the second week of May is better than the first. They often start a second brood before the young ones have left the spot, so if you see them flying about, and no old hen with them, she is very likely sitting on a fresh lot somewhere near.

5.—THE ROBIN (Fig. 7).

Bird.—I need not say much about him. You must know his song, which he sings all the year round; and the way he will come into the house in cold weather; but not everyone knows that he is a most bloodthirsty fighter. Most Robins migrate like other birds, but I think those that make friends with people stay all the year round.

Nesting-place.—A hole in a bank is the favourite place for a Robin's nest, but they quite often use old tins, boots, flower-pots and other shelters. You will seldom find one in a place where the rain can get into it.

Nest.—A Robin builds the front of her nest first, almost always of dead leaves packed in very cleverly to look like any other collection of leaves that have drifted into a hole during the Winter. This may deceive her *enemies*, but gives the secret away to the experienced birdsnester, who has learnt to look out for that very thing.

The nest-cup is well behind this rampart and fairly deep, so that you can rarely see the eggs; in fact the scheme is the same as the Wagtails have. The body of the nest is moss and roots, and the lining mostly fine roots with very little hair.

Eggs.—The eggs are very large for the size of the bird, generally six or seven, whitish, with markings very like the freckles on your nose, if you are that sort of person. You will hardly mistake them for a spotted Flycatcher's, which are much more blotchy.

Young.—You may have wondered why I put the Robin down as a near relation of the true Thrushes, but I think when you see the speckled young ones you will understand. *And* watch his wings and tail as he hops about.

Season.—You may find an occasional nest in March and a good many in the first week of April in an average year. Early June is when most of the second broods are going—I once found one of them in the top of a clipped hedge, like a Hedge Sparrow's nest.

6.—THE NIGHTINGALE.

He has nested in Northumberland—once—but you won't find one north of Sheffield, as a rule. Those that are mentioned in the papers, singing at such and such a place, generally turn out to be Sedge Warblers.

Bird.—He is a dingy-looking little bird, and you are not likely to recognize him if you see him. You can't mistake his song at night (if you know a Sedge-Warbler's) but in the daytime it is harder to pick out among all the other birds.

Haunts.—His favourite haunt is a strip of wood, with good undergrowth, or a shrubbery; and his nest is on the ground, in various sorts of places, but always well hidden.

Nest.—It will show you that he is a near relation of the Robin's for it is a very similar affair, with even more dead leaves about it.

Eggs.—The five eggs are *dark* olive-brown, and not like any others; though there is one variety which shows some of the ground colour, light blue or green.

Young.—The young ones are speckled, rather like young Robins.

Season.—The nesting-time is June, or perhaps the very end of May right in the south.

7.—THE REDSTART.

Or " Firetail."

Bird.—The cock is easy to recognize. He has a black mask across eyes, beak and throat, and is bluish above and reddish below, with a red tail which he flirts from side to side. The hen is a quiet-looking brown bird, but with the same red tail, which you can see as she sits on the nest or as she flies away.

Haunts.—They are Summer birds, and arrive rather late. They are not common, but are scattered about all over the place, perhaps most often about gardens, but sometimes miles from a house.

They nest in holes, in walls or buildings for choice, but in trees as well. Limekilns are good places, and I have found them in banks faced with stone. One of this kind I remember was a long way in, and took the whole length of my arm (not quite so long then as it is now); but as a rule they are quite easy to get at.

Nest.—The nest is made of grass and moss and lined with lots of feathers; loose as a rule, but in a big hole neatly built in one corner, not spread about as some hole-builders would do.

Habits.—The bird sits very tight, and I have known one let me pull out a stone, take her photograph, and put the stone back, without moving; but if the nest is an open one, she generally flicks off as you approach.

Eggs.—The eggs are often six or more, pale blue with a greenish tinge and a very polished shell, which will help you to distinguish them from Hedge Sparrows', but *not* from Pied Flycatchers'.

I *once* found a nest where all the eggs were lightly dusted with small dark specks, but I think this is very unusual.

Season.—Redstarts seldom have eggs much before June.

8.—THE WHEATEAR.

Often called " Stone-chat " and " White Rump."

Bird.—Both his local names hit him off very well; for he haunts stone walls, " chat " is his note which you can imitate by knocking two pebbles together, and he is always showing off the white patch on his rump and the base of his tail as he flits along the wall in front of you. I believe the " Wheatear " is old English for " White

Fig. 11—Blackcap
(see page 93)

Fig. 12.—Spotted Flycatcher
(see page 102)

tail" and has nothing to do with corn. His colour is grey and white, picked out with black, and you can't mistake him.

Haunts.—He goes to Africa for the Winter, but gets back here very early in April, or even before. The best place for him is up in the hills, where the fences are all stone walls, and even further out where there are no walls; but a few are to be found lower down too, about quarries or sand pits or river banks.

Nest.—The nest is in a hole in a wall where there is such a thing, but may be found in a hole in a sand-bank or peat-hag, and I *have* seen one on the ground under a bush, like a Whinchat's. Wherever it is it is right out of sight, and very hard to find, especially in a dry wall with as many holes as stones in it. If you are hunting for the nest you must look out for the slightest signs, and if you are watching the birds you will need all your patience or they will beat you.

The nest is made chiefly of grass, loosely built, and lined with feathers, wool or hair.

Eggs.—The eggs are generally six, very pale blue and rather large, and when once you have seen them they are easy enough to distinguish from other blue eggs.

Season.—Some may be found quite early in May, and they should all be sitting by the third week.

9.—THE WHINCHAT.

Bird.—He is a little stumpy bird with a speckled back and fawn coloured breast; you can recognize him best by his head, which looks nearly black, with a strong white streak over the eye. The hen is the same, but quieter-coloured, and they both sit about on the top of low bushes, trees or railings and make the family noise, like the clink of stones, twitching their tails as they do it. The cock has a pretty song, but does not sing a great deal.

You see them both before the eggs are laid and after they are hatched, but in between they are so shy that you may very well think they have left the place altogether, and not find out your mistake till it is too late for eggs.

Haunts.—Their favourite haunts are young fir plantations, where the trees are not much taller than the grass, and bushy places generally; but I have seen nests by the roadside, or in a tuft of grass in a rough field, not far from the fence. They may be in all sorts of places, but *whins* are the least likely, in spite of the name.

Nest.—The nest is always on the ground, and very well hidden, perhaps right under a bush and with a little tunnel through the grass leading to it. In any case the bird seldom flies straight in, but settles a little way off like a Lark and runs in.

This makes it very hard to find by watching the birds, as you cannot often get near enough to see just where they go, and they are very wary besides. Once on the nest they sit fairly well, and you might find it by making a rush straight for the spot where she disappeared. If that fails you had better go back about dusk and poke about quietly on the chance of disturbing her after she has settled down for the night.

Eggs.—The nest is built chiefly of grass, and lined with hair, and the eggs, generally five, are *dark* blue with faint brown markings, which often look like a stain just below the surface. The shell is glossy like a Redstart's.

Season.—Late May and early June are the times to look for a Whinchat's nest, as he is one of the late-comers.

10.—THE STONECHAT.

Bird.—The cock bird is easy to recognize, having the whole of his head black except for a white patch on each side of the neck. His back is dark, with a little white above the tail, his breast dull-red, and his wings show a good white patch. The hen is very like him, with all colours duller.

Haunts.—You sometimes see a Stonechat or two in winter, so he is a hardier bird than the last three, which all find Europe too cold. But even in summer he is much rarer than the Whinchat. The likeliest place to find them is a common with plenty of whin or other bushes scattered about, and they seem to prefer high ground. You can hardly help seeing the birds if they are there, for they sit about on bushes and " chack " at you like Whinchats. " Whinchat " would be quite a good name for this bird, and you can always look out for him where there are whins.

Nest.—The nest is always on the ground or very near it. It is built just like a Whinchat's, but may have various kinds of lining stuff. It is just as hard to find, too, and if you are watching the birds, mind you keep your eye on the *hen*.

Eggs.—The eggs are generally five, and are like a Whinchat's, only the blue is lighter and the brown darker and more distinct. Even when there are *no* markings (as happens occasionally) the blue is the same, and the nest can only be one of the two. A Wheatear would never nest in that sort of place, *and* its eggs are always bigger, and not the same blue.

Season.—As you would expect, they nest much earlier than Whinchats, perhaps even at the end of April, and often have second broods.

II.—THE HEDGE SPARROW.

"Smoky" or "Shuffle-wing" in the North, and often "Hedge Accentor" in books.

Of course you know by now that he is a soft-billed bird, and no more a "Sparrow" than a Nightingale is; I expect he got his name through being so common and so tame. I need not tell you what he looks like, but I advise you to be sure you know his song, which you can hear any fine day in February. It is only when you notice all the common birds' songs that you are likely to spot something better, such as a Wood Wren or a Lesser Whitethroat.

This is one of the few birds that seem to be common in Winter as well as in Summer, but for all that I believe he migrates like the rest. See if you can find out this way: Count how many you see on a certain walk in January, again in February, and again in March. That ought to give you a good idea, as they are about the hedges at all times of the year.

The Hedge Sparrow's haunts you know, its nest you can study for yourselves, and its eggs are so blue and have so little gloss on them that you can always distinguish them from the other blue eggs.

Season.—Some are often laying by the end of March; and the second nests are always worth looking into for a Cuckoo's egg, in June.

FAMILY VI.
II.—THE WARBLERS.

You might have expected to find the Nightingale among them, but I have shown you that his proper place is next to the Robin.

These are all very small birds, and most of them pretty singers, as their name will tell you. They all leave England in Autumn, except one, and most of them leave Europe as well. Most of them are very hard to know by sight, so you need to know their songs. As a rule they arrive towards the end of April, and the last week in May and the first in June will be a busy time with their nests. One brood is the rule with them, though in a good year they sometimes rear a second brood. The first three build domed nests, but the rest are open, and very flimsy affairs in a good many cases. They all build low down, on the ground or within reach of it. Don't forget they really belong to the big Thrush Family.

I.—THE WILLOW WREN (Fig. 8).

Bird.—This is a graceful little bird, light olive green above and yellowish-white below, with a habit of running up the branches, pecking as he goes, but in a very different way from the Tits. His song is very simple and very sweet, just a descending scale like the Chaffinch's, but the notes soft and mellow. You probably know it already, for he is the commonest of all the Warblers.

Haunts.—Willow-wrens arrive in shoals about the middle of April, and spread themselves all over the countryside. Their nests may be anywhere about the woods and hedge-sides, and are nearly always on the ground. Favourite places are hedge-banks and sides of ditches, but you will even find them in the open field, though generally under the shelter of some old thorn branch; and where there are small scrubby bushes they often build under them.

Nest.—The nest has a domed roof which overhangs a little in front, and the opening is wide, and so low down that the eggs can nearly always be seen from outside. It is built of grass, moss, and dead leaves, and lined with so many feathers that North-country people call the birds "Feather-pokes."

Habits.—The bird sits closely and slips off very quietly. You can't always see just where she comes from, and may have some trouble in finding the nest, though you have seen her going away. If you look first just by your feet and then where your stick was, you ought to find it, as you were probably nearly touching the nest before she went.

You can find Willow Wrens' nests by keeping still and watching, but it needs a good deal of patience. If you do try it, your experience will be useful when you come to watch for either of the next two birds, whose ways are much the same.

Eggs.—Six or seven eggs are laid, pure white with red markings, which vary a good deal in size and shade, and are more like dabs from the point of a brush than spots, and too small to call blotches. They are sometimes dark red-brown, but not often. If you find a nest regularly about the same spot, you should take an egg every year, and you will soon see whether they are laid by the same bird, by their markings.

Season.—You will find the first nests in the third week of May as a rule.

2.—CHIFF-CHAFF.

Bird.—This bird is so like the Willow Wren that you have to know a lot to tell which is which if you have them in your hand. Luckily its song is quite easy, just two notes *of the same length* repeated sleepily like this: "Chiff-chaff-chaff-chiff," perhaps for hours together.

WARBLERS.

Don't mistake the Great Tit's saw-sharpening note for this bird's. It goes this way: " Chiff-cháff, chiff-cháff," and much quicker, but it does *suggest* chiff-chaff, if you only know the bird's name.

Migration.—It gets rarer as you go North, and is quite rare in many parts of Northumberland, and as a few winter in Cornwall and Devon, some of the birds must not shift their quarters more than 600 miles or so, a very short journey compared with what some of the other Warblers do.

Haunts.—Woods and orchards are likeliest places for a chiff-chaff, but wherever you hear one singing (and he sticks to the same tree) there is the place to look for the nest.

Nest.—It is very seldom *on* the ground, but often not far above it, among the undergrowth; or in ivy, perhaps some way up the wall or tree; or even once in a way in a low bush.

It is made of the same sort of stuff as the Willow Wren's, with perhaps more grass and leaves and less moss, but the shape is different. It is deeper and more oval, and the hole is small and near the top, instead of wide and below the middle. The lining is the same, chiefly feathers.

A Tip.—If you know where one sings regularly, you might try this dodge to find its nest. Take some white feathers and scatter them in the open near the spot, in the evening; and come back early next morning and watch. If the bird is building she is sure to come and carry them off, and you must be a duffer if you can't see where she takes them to. Try it a day or two before May 1st, and if nobody comes, keep an eye on the spot, and when the feathers begin to disappear, try again. If your bird is very late in beginning you will perhaps find several Willow Wrens coming for feathers, too, but she *ought* to have eggs by the time they begin to build.

Eggs.—The eggs are rather like the Willow Wren's, but as a rule the markings are *spots*, clean-cut and dark, and rather fewer of them; and they often have some pale greyish undermarkings, which I have never noticed in Willow Wrens' eggs. Still, it is easy to make a mistake in the case of pale Chiff-Chaffs' and dark Willow Wrens', and the nest is the best guide.

Season.—The birds should arrive within a day or two of April 1st, so soon after May 1st is the time to expect eggs, but they are often later. They are said to have two broods sometimes, but I think only in the South.

3.—THE WOOD WREN.

Bird.—You can tell it from a Willow Wren by its much yellower look, and you should try to get to know its loud shivering song, which is pitched on about the same note as a Wren's, but begins with a twitter of about 8 to 12 notes, just slow enough to count, and then breaks into a trill, lasting rather longer and much too fast to count. When he *is* singing he gives you plenty of it, about 8 times to the minute, but the best time to hear him is in the morning, as he very rarely sings after mid-day. He also has a call-note, a loud " Twee twee twee " repeated six or seven times, which is just as easy to recognize as his song. Unlike most birds, he seems to sing just as much when he is feeding a family of young ones as at other times.

Haunts.—This bird is rare all over England, and only favours certain parts, but I know the Tyne valley is one of them.

Its lowland haunts are tall woods, of beech for choice and I think you are more likely to find the nest in places where there is not too much thick undergrowth. It does not keep only to the low country, like a Chiff-chaff, but may also be found well up the hill-sides, in fact as near the moors as the trees go, and it is easier to find a nest in a little clump of birches up there than in the big woods lower down.

Nest.—The nest is always on the ground, often in a bank or at the roots of a tree, and hidden by a tuft of grass as a rule, though it may be found in a tangle of undergrowth, or in heather, etc. It is very like a Willow Wren's, with a wide opening, though I think it is a little deeper, the eggs more out of sight. It is made of much the same sort of stuff outside, but *never* lined with feathers, just fine grass and perhaps a little hair.

Habits.—The bird's habits are very like the Willow Wren's, so that you can often find her at home. If you see two of them about keep still and watch, and you ought to find the nest with patience.

Eggs.—The six eggs are white with small dark brown spots, about twice as many as on the average Willow Wren's, and you can hardly mistake them.

Season.—The birds come rather late, and June 1st is soon enough to look for eggs. But you can hear their song from early May onwards, and have a good idea where to look.

4.—THE WHITETHROAT (Fig. 9).
Or " Nettle-Creeper."

Bird.—The chief difference you will see between him and the Willow Wren is his rather dark head and back, helping to show up his white throat. You must be near him to see that the throat is any lighter than the breast.

His song is short and hurried and very cheery, and you hear it most when he first comes in April. He sings on a telegraph wire or the top of the hedge, and also on the wing, but in between he keeps diving into the hedge, where he jumps from twig to twig, twisting in and out and never still, except when he hops up to sing his little song again.

Haunts.—He is a common bird everywhere, and his haunts are hedges, woods and thickets. His nest is hardly ever *in* the hedge; he prefers the thick growth alongside it, nettles or goosegrass or any old weed will do so long as it is thick. Brambles are another favourite haunt, and there is no better place for most of the Warblers than an open sort of wood with plenty of sun and bramble-clumps, or a narrow lane where the hedges are overgrown with them.

Nest.—The nest is always low down, naturally, and sometimes right on the ground; but most often it hangs from its support, instead of resting on it. It is very flimsy, and very deep, sometimes as much as $3\frac{1}{2}$ inches, made of thin grass stalks and lined with a little horsehair. It is more like network than weaving, and you can nearly always see through the sides.

To Find It.—The best way to find the nest is to poke about with a stick till you flush the bird. Afterwards the two of them will hop about in the bushes near you, giving a sort of scolding note which will warn you to look for the nest even if you have not seen the bird go away.

Eggs.—The eggs are five or occasionally six. Their general colour is cloudy green with darker markings, which vary a good deal. You will soon get to know them pretty well. Most of the markings seem to be just under the surface, and eggs with dark markings on top are rare. The deep nest will help you to recognize any eggs that are out of the common.

Season.—The first nests are ready soon after the middle of May; but if you are making an expedition to some special haunt, the first days of June will be best as you will have a better chance of some of the rarer Warblers, and there will still be plenty of Whitethroats.

5.—THE LESSER WHITETHROAT (Fig. 10).

Bird.—This bird is rather darker than a Whitethroat, but the only good way to distinguish them is by the song, which is very short, ending with " sip, sip, sip," and repeated over and over again.

Haunts.—It is very much rarer than the Whitethroat, but once you have found one, you are pretty sure to find a nest about the same spot every year. Its haunts are woods and hedges, too, but more often woods, and all the nests I have found have been much higher up than a Whitethroat ever builds, even up to eight feet. I have seen them in small fir trees and evergreens, but perhaps the favourite place is in the hedge round a wood.

Nest.—The nest is built like a Whitethroat's, but is smaller, shallower, and very neatly shaped—it is like a little bowl, while the other is like a bag, and when you have seen one you can always recognize them afterwards.

I have never known them to have any hair lining, but this may not be always the rule.

The birds sit closely, and when disturbed make rather less fuss than Whitethroats.

Eggs.—The eggs are four or five, with a clear white or cream ground colour, and darker markings which vary a good deal, often two shades of brown in blotches or spots, but with a greenish tinge to remind you of the Whitethroat. You can't mistake them.

Season.—Any time from the middle of May to the end. Second broods not uncommon.

6.—THE GARDEN WARBLER.

Bird.—This bird is a richer brown colour than most of them, but not easy to distinguish by eye. By ear it is much easier for he sings all day, a bubbling sort of song which is sure to catch your ear. I can't describe it, but he is the happiest sounding of all, and has a wonderfully sweet tone.

Haunts.—Not as common as the Whitethroat, but by no means rare. You *may* find him in gardens, nesting in a gooseberry-bush for choice, but woods are his favourite haunt, and brambles his nesting-place.

Nest.—The nest is on the same plan as a Whitethroat's, and built of the same stuff, though often without any hair lining; and it is much more solidly built and shallower. It doesn't remind you of network at all, and is nearly always supported by a bush or branch of some sort, not slung on to nettles or other weeds, even when built among them. I have never seen one right on the ground.

It is often very little hidden, and you may see the bird on the nest; she is reddish-brown, and often has a faint pale streak over the eye. They behave very like Whitethroats, and have the same scolding note.

Eggs.—The four or five eggs are of many kinds, and you can get quite a good collection of them without having two alike. The ground colour varies from white to pale brown; the markings are of several shades of brown and grey, laid on in spots, blotches, or streaks, hard to describe, but easy to recognize. They are rather larger than most of the Warblers', and can only be confused with the Blackcap's.

Season.—Rather late, seldom before June.

7.—THE BLACKCAP (Fig. 11).

Bird.—This is one of the Warblers you may know by sight, by his black cap and his greyish back (only don't mix him up with the Marsh Tit, whose cap reaches to the back of his neck, and who has white cheek-patches that nearly meet behind). The hen bird has a reddish-brown cap and a browner back, but you should be able to know her from a Garden Warbler if you see her on the nest. The cock bird has a beautiful song, like the Garden Warbler's, but more varied and louder, and you hear him a good deal more often than you see him.

Haunts.—They haunt the same sorts of places as Garden Warblers, but are much less common in the North. Brambles are their favourite cover, but I have found nests in thickets of blackthorn and in shrubberies. If you know the song you will know where to look.

Nest.—The nest is even more flimsy than a Whitethroat's at times, but not deep, more like a round hammock. I saw one in France, slung between two twigs of an elder branch, the bottom of which was really only a few horse-hairs crossing each other; and one windy day the eggs all slipped through! I often used to see the cock bird sitting on that nest, and once heard him singing as he sat; so if you find a nest, you should soon learn to know the Blackcap's song.

Eggs.—The eggs, four or five, are very like the Garden Warbler's, but many of them have a brick-red tinge which that bird never has. The way the nest is built is generally enough to settle the matter, and you should see the birds as they hop about and scold you; but if you go to the nest once or twice in the late afternoon or evening you will very likely see the cock bird on, and if he is a Blackcap, one glimpse will tell you so.

Season.—You are not likely to find them before June.

Note.—Now I have told you enough for you to see the value of knowing the songs of different Warblers. If you can get someone who knows them all to go with you to a likely haunt some time in May, and give you a lesson, it will help you a lot; if not, I advise you whenever you find a fresh one, to hang about near the spot and make the *bird* give you a lesson. And if you keep quiet you have a good chance of finding other nests while you are waiting.

8.—THE REED WARBLER.

Bird.—A bird you very seldom see, but they are always chattering incessantly among the reeds, and there is no mistaking when they are there.

Haunts.—They are common where reeds grow (not rushes), but there are not many reed-beds in the North, so you are not likely to find them North of Yorkshire.

Nest.—The nest is very deep indeed, and built round the stems of three or four reeds, often as soon as they are a foot or so high, but I have seen it as high as my head.

Eggs.—The eggs are whitish with a lot of dark blotches, and like no other bird's except the Marsh Warbler's, which is *very* rare and never builds in reeds.

Season.—The time depends on when the Reeds begin to grow, which is often very late. But they sometimes nest in last year's reeds, where they have not been cut, and you may see nests close up to the feathery tops. Cuckoos are fond of putting their eggs into these nests when they are low down and close to the bank, and I have seen two in one nest, and a third in another not 20 yards away. You can look for them in June some time.

9.—THE MARSH WARBLER.

This is one of the rarest British birds, only known to nest regularly in Somerset. It is very like the Reed Warbler in all ways except that it never builds its nest in the reeds, but always over the land, in some bush. The nest is not quite so deep, and the eggs have a clearer white ground-colour.

10.—THE SEDGE WARBLER.

Bird.—A little restless sharp-looking bird, with a light streak over the eye, rather difficult to get a good look at; but you can hear him singing at any time of the day or night, if you go near enough to his haunt to disturb him. His North-country name is "Chitterchat," and if you know that name you will recognize his song all right; it is an angry-sounding twittering business, with a note every now and then that is like a Sparrow's, and at night you can hear him saying quite distinctly "Get-away-to-bed, Get-away-to-bed."

Haunts.—You will always find Sedge Warblers in Willow thickets near the river, or in a scrubby marsh by a lake; but nests are often to be found in bushy places, young coverts and hedges a good way from any water.

Place.—Down in Wicken Fen, where the Swallow-tail Butterflies live, they often build among the tall sedge, but in the North I always find the nests in bushes, sometimes quite high up.

Nest.—Some nests are slight, but more often they are rather bulky; loosely made of grass, moss, etc., and lined with hair or down or both.

The bird is apt to slip away without being seen, and you have to look for the nest itself. In willows you can find it easily, and only need look at the bushes that have suitable forks, mostly sallows; but I have seen it cunningly hidden in a clump of drift stuff left among the branches by the floods.

Eggs.—The four or five eggs are mottled all over with pale brown, with generally a black streak or two. You cannot confuse them with any other Warbler's, but they are very like a Grey Wagtail's.

Season.—They don't often lay before June.

II.—THE GRASSHOPPER WARBLER.

Bird.—This is the only Warbler with a speckled head and back, and the throat is speckled too, but you will seldom get a look at him, he is so shy. However, you can tell when he is about by his song, just like a Grasshopper, or someone winding up a watch, but louder of course. He sings most of the night, but not much in the day-time.

Fig. 13—Goldcrest
(see page 115)

Fig. 14—Greater Spotted Woodpecker

(*see page* 118)

Haunts.—He is a rare bird, and does not come back to the same place every year; so if you hear him, you should have a good try for the nest. His favourite haunts are young coverts where the trees are not more than shoulder high, with plenty of long grass, and hedge-bottoms with the same; but he has been known to nest on the heather right up to the Cheviots, and there you *could* get a look at him.

Nest.—The nest is always on the ground or very near it, well hidden, made of grass and a very little moss. It is solid and deep, and has no lining but grass.

The bird sits well, and slips off very quietly; if you get a look at her, you will notice her rounded tail.

Eggs.—The eggs are any number up to seven, pinkish white, and dusted pretty thickly with small brown spots; rather like a Willow Wren's, but hardly to be mistaken. The open nest, with its grass lining, will tell you what they are.

Season.—At the end of May, or in June.

12.—THE DARTFORD WARBLER.

Called " Furze Wren " in the South.

The bird is dark grey on top, chestnut below, and has a long fan-shaped tail with white outer edges, so is rather unlike the other Warblers.

Haunts.—It only lives in one corner of England, South of the Humber and East of the Severn, and seems not to migrate at all, living all the year round among the gorse where it nests. So you have small hopes of finding any stragglers in the North.

Nest, Etc.—It does not build in the bush as a rule, but in long heather or other growth under a spray of gorse. The nest and eggs are very like a Whitethroat's, and two broods are reared, in April and June.

That is the end of the Thrush family, and the next has only one British bird in it.

VII.—THE DIPPER.

Called in the North " Water Ousel " or " Water Crow."

Bird.—He is like a stumpy sort of Blackbird with a white waistcoat and a short tail which he cocks up in the air at times. He flies straight and low over the water, chirping as he goes, and curtseys as he sits on a stone. He sings all the Winter, in or out of the water, a cheerful little song rather like a Robin's, but more lively.

The funny thing about a Dipper is that with feet just like a Thrush he can dive and swim, *and* stay at the bottom. If you have ever tried it in a swimming-bath you know how hard it is, and a bird is three times as buoyant as you are. It looks like a miracle, but I suppose he must be swimming downwards with his wings all the time.

Haunts.—He is a common bird in his own haunts, which are burns, and fast-flowing rivers, and a fair number are to be seen all the year round. I cannot say whether there are any new arrivals in Spring, but I rather think not.

Nesting-place.—The favourite nesting-place is a ledge or crevice in the mossy face of a waterfall quite often in behind the water; after that comes a bridge, where the nest is often on one of the beams or girders; and you sometimes find a nest on top of a big boulder in midstream. But wherever it is 99 times out of 100 it is placed so that the young ones can jump straight out into the water.

I have seen one in the side of Gaping Ghyll hole on Ingleboro', and the young ones *could* jump into the water there, though I don't suppose they often do, as they would hit it some 300 feet below, and not see the light again till the stream washed them out at the cave, 1,000 feet or so lower down!

Nest.—It is made in two parts. The outside is a flat-topped dome of moss, which overhangs the entrance. This is finished first, and is often very big, say a foot from back to front. Inside is a nest very like a Blackbird's lined with dead leaves, which keep the eggs dry, however wet the outside of the nest may be. I have seen one in Wensleydale which was not only wet, but had all the moss part turned to stone by the drip from a spring. The birds used it every year, and I dare say they are using it still.

About those dead leaves—if you should ever find a nest up a hill burn and a mile or more from the nearest tree, look carefully and see whether the birds go all that way to fetch them, or use something else.

Eggs.—The eggs are five or six and pure white, with a dull surface and a very thin shell.

Season.—Dippers begin to build very early in March, but you won't often find eggs before the 20th unless, perhaps, in an old nest that needed very little rebuilding. A second brood is often reared in the same nest.

VIII.—THE WREN.

Another family with only one British bird, and a common one. He is like the Dipper in shape and in the way he cocks his tail, and has the same good habit of singing in Winter, and a much finer song for his size.

Nesting-place.—The Wren's haunts are everywhere, and its nesting-places as varied as its haunts. The favourite is among the roots of a tree, whether undermined by water or uprooted by the wind, and the second-best, ivy on a wall or tree. It is often built in a small well-clipped hedge, or in any kind of crevice or cranny in wood or stone. Other places I have known are under clumps of grass or fern growing out of a wall, in a branch of a larch tree, in the side of a haystack, under a Thrush's nest (with eggs, too) in some ivy, in a Swallow's nest, and in the carcase of a Carrion Crow (hanging up).

Nest.—The nest is oval, sometimes nearly round, sometimes very deep, and is made chiefly of moss as a rule, but generally camouflaged with dead leaves or something of the sort. This part varies according to where the nest is, and is very interesting to study. I have seen one apparently made of nothing but straw, and another of honeysuckle bark, which had a very fine effect.

The hole in the side is very small, and strengthened with grass or twigs woven into the moss. One finger is about all you can get in without straining it, and some say that if you touch it before the lining of hair and feathers is in, the bird is very apt to desert.

Deserting.—I don't think this is true myself, for I saw a Wren trying to build on a girder in an unfinished house, and, as the ceiling would have shut it off from the world in a day or two, pulled out what she had done several times; but she kept coming back and starting again, bringing leaves and moss and building furiously, in spite of people working or standing watching her, until she was finally shut out. That doesn't look like deserting easily, and I think all the nests that are supposed to have been deserted were what are called " cock nests."

"Cock Nests."—These are supposed to be built by the cock to occupy his spare time while the hen is building the proper nest, and are just the same except for the lining, which is left out. Of course you can't tell the cock from the hen, but I have two reasons for believing in this theory besides what I have said already. First, I have seen Wrens building often enough, but I have never seen two birds at work on one nest; second, I have found " cock nests " in very out-of-the-way places, where it was *most* unlikely that any human being could have disturbed them. That's all I know about it, but *you* may be able to settle the question, if you should ever see the two Wrens at once building separate nests, and find afterwards that one was used and the other deserted.

These birds sit pretty close on their eggs, and will bite your finger if you shove it in while they are at home, though they usually fly off before it comes to that.

Eggs.—Six eggs is the average number, large for the bird, and white with pinkish spots, like the Tits'.

Season.—You may find the first brood about the end of April, the second in June.

The rest of the Perchers are birds which you will not see either walking or hopping, though no doubt they do one or the other at times, most likely hop. They are the Flycatchers, Swallows, Shrikes and Tits.

FAMILY IX.
THE FLYCATCHERS.

Their way of feeding is to choose a perch with a good open space round it, where they solemnly sit till an insect comes by within easy range; then they give chase, generally catch it, and go back to the perch to wait for the next. It is easy to recognize them by this habit, so I need say no more about them. We only have two.

I.—THE SPOTTED FLYCATCHER (Fig. 12).

Bird.—A little grey-looking bird which you will know best by his way of catching flies. You *can* see the spots at about six feet away, on the head and throat. He has a quiet little call-note, but doesn't sing.

Haunts.—He is one of the later Summer birds, and is very fond of gardens. You may also find him round the edges of woods, in clumps of trees in the open, and sometimes along the hedges, but not often; I think only when extra large numbers turn up and all the favourite places are taken.

Nesting-place.—The nest is always built against something solid, wall or tree, and seldom in a real hole. The likeliest place is in ivy on a wall, often within reach but never very low; ivy on a tree is another favourite place, and you will often find them built against a bare trunk, supported by some little bump, or even clinging to the rough bark like a bracket. But they prefer a shallow sort of niche if they can get one.

Nest.—The outside is of moss, wool, cobwebs and grass, but I have seen it made entirely of the inner bark of trees; the lining is sometimes made of nothing but strips of the same, but more often hair and feathers.

The nest is very small, and without the eggs you may know it by the outer part being not round, but horseshoe shaped, the stone or bark forming the back. As the bird builds either in a shallow recess or no recess at all, she wants the nest to stick out as little as possible.

The only *round* Flycatcher's nest I remember seeing was built plumb in the middle of an old Blackbird's nest up in the broken top of an old elm tree.

I have seen two new nests within six inches of one another on an ivy-covered wall. They were exactly alike, lined out properly and ready for eggs, but I never found anything in either. Another mystery!

Eggs.—The eggs are four or five, very pale blue with dull red blotches. If the red is scarce you may take them for Robins' at first sight, but the ground colour is always different.

Season.—Generally early June, very rarely in May.

2.—THE PIED FLYCATCHER.

Bird.—This bird is *much* rarer than the last, but if you come across a pair you are sure to notice them. They are black above, except for a white forehead and a patch on each wing, and all white below. At a distance you might take one for a Chaffinch, which sometimes takes flies in the same way, but there is no mistaking it if you are within 50 yards.

Haunts and Nest.—They nearly always nest in open woods, often by a stream, and the nest is always in a hole. I believe they have been known to use a hole in a wall or a cliff, but a tree is the usual thing. Any kind of hole will do, though they seem to like one with a wide opening best. The nest is loosely made of grass, moss, dead leaves, etc., and lined with anything soft.

Eggs.—The eggs may be any number up to 9, and are pale blue, just like a Redstart's. So if you find such a nest and see no birds, it is impossible to tell which it is, though a lot of feathers generally means a Redstart.

Season.—May or early June is the time for eggs.

FAMILY X.
THE SWALLOWS.

Everybody knows the look of these birds, with their long wings, forked tail, and swift flight. Their feet have nearly gone out of use and are very small and weak, and that is why they like to perch on wires, thin twigs, and the edges of spouts. They all get their living by catching insects on the wing, and their mouths have a wide gape accordingly. They all go to Africa for the winter and yet find time to rear two broods, so they have a busy time of it.

I.—THE SWALLOW.

Bird.—In flight you may know the Swallow from above by his glossy dark-blue back, from below by his round-forked tail with long pointed outer feathers. Close to, you will see his red throat with a black collar below it. He has a very pretty song, which you may hear very early in the morning, before the other birds begin.

Haunts.—Barns, stables and hay-sheds are favourite places with Swallows, and they are always fond of "hemmels" and sheds out in the fields, far away from any house.

Nest.—The nest is inside a building as a rule, though you occasionally see one outside, in a sheltered place. It is nearly always supported by something, though it *may* be just plastered on to the wall.

It is made of mud, little pellets built up like bricks, and seldom more than three inches high, generally more like a saucer than a cup; and is always open round the top. The lining is a little straw or grass, and some feathers.

We had a nest once which burst when the young ones were growing up; we put the whole lot inside an old cap, and the birds not only brought off their brood safely, but laid a second lot of eggs in the cap afterwards.

Eggs.—Five or six is the usual number, pure white with markings from rusty to dark brown, in spots or blotches, so that a good many varieties can be got. You can easily tell one bird's from another's, and if you know two or three nests that are used every year, and take an egg from each and keep them carefully, you can tell pretty certainly after a year or two whether the *same birds* come back to them or not.

Season.—May 20th is soon enough to look for eggs, and I have found them as late as August. They do not always hatch their second broods, but I think they always make a start.

2.—THE HOUSE MARTIN.
Or "Window Swallow."

Bird.—If he is flying below you, you can see that the lower half of his back is *white;* above you, he shows a straight-cut fork in his tail, and is all white up to the chin. If you see him at the edge of a pond or puddle, picking up mud for building, you will notice his white feet and legs, which are feathered right down to the toes, like a Grouse's.

Haunts.—These birds are not to be found everywhere, like Swallows, but a good many nests are generally built on a house that they have taken a fancy to.

In some places great colonies of Martins build on the cliffs, and no doubt they all did that before *we* got civilized enough to build houses for them.

Nest.—The nest is always on the outside of the House, under the eaves or in the top corner of a window, though a good many are built *in* hay-sheds under the highest part of the roof; it is built of mud pellets like a Swallow's, with these differences. It very seldom has any support below, it is a big affair, like half a turnip in shape, and is built right up to the roof all round, with a little gap left at some point for the birds to get in and out. The lining is like the Swallow's, and the nest must get very hot inside, with its brick walls and only one small opening high up.

Martins like to come back to their old nests just as Swallows do, but they very often find Sparrows in possession. The Sparrows will even take their new nests from them, and throw the eggs or young ones out.

Eggs.—They lay four or five pure white eggs, rather smaller than a Swallow's.

Season.—They appear a few days after the Swallows, but they generally have to build a new nest, and it takes a long time, so you won't often find eggs before June. I have found them in September, second broods, of course, or perhaps third. These would never be hatched, or at any rate the young would not be reared.

3.—THE SAND MARTIN.

Bird.—A Sand Martin is the same sort of shape as the other two, but brown, and a little smaller. He has the same twittering kind of note, but I have never heard him sing, as a Swallow does.

Haunts.—They are common birds, but you don't see many far away from their haunts, which are river-

SWALLOWS—SHRIKES.

banks, or other sandy places such as railway-cuttings or sand-pits. There you will often see hundreds together.

Nest.—They dig a burrow into the cliff or bank, perhaps a yard long and of a flattened oval shape, the height less than the width; and the nest is in a sort of chamber at the end, lined with a few straws and feathers. How they dig out with their little soft bills is one of the mysteries, but you will notice that it is only certain soft layers of sand that suit them.

I have seen them using narrow drain-pipes to nest in at Cambridge, but I expect the first heavy rain gave them a bit of a shock.

Eggs.—The eggs are usually six, pure white and rather smaller than a House Martin's and have very thin shells.

Season.—They come early, sometimes even before the end of March, and if they can get to work at once you may find eggs in the first week of May; but if the river has been washing away the bank and they have to dig new burrows it will be more like June—and second broods accordingly, but often early in July.

Note.—If you see a Sand Martin take a feather into her nest it does not always mean she has not laid yet, for they often add them later.

FAMILY XI.—THE SHRIKES.

These are curious birds. Insect-feeders by nature, which have taken to feeding on bigger game, and have just the beginnings of the hooked beak and claws of the birds of prey. They can't kill their victims decently, like a hawk, but drag them off to their larder, where they stick them on thorns, setting up a regular butcher's shop, from which they get their name of "Butcher-birds."

Only one of them nests in England, and he only in the South.

THE RED-BACKED SHRIKE.

Bird.—He is about the size of a Lark, and reminds you of an executioner, with a black mask across his eyes. His head is grey, his back chestnut, his breast pinkish, and he has a long fanshaped tail, black and white, which he is always flicking up and down. His mate is chiefly brown, barred with black.

Haunts.—He lives among fields and lanes, where there are tall hedges and thorn-bushes, in which he likes to nest.

Nest.—The nest is generally high up, say eight feet, and is easy to see; for it is big and loosely built of grass, roots, a few twigs, moss, wool and hair, or some of these things. You know where to look, for you are sure to see the cock-bird sitting near by, on a post or stump or the top of a bush, making strange noises and flicking his tail.

Eggs.—The four or five eggs are rather less than a Lark's whitish, with spots of brown and grey, generally in a ring; and they vary a great deal.

Season.—The first week in June is the time for them.

FAMILY XII.
THE TITS or TIT-MICE.

You must know some of these birds, with their dark heads and white cheek-patches, their acrobatic climbing tricks, and their funny little calls. You *may* learn to know the different Tits by their voices, but very few people can. Cock and hen are exactly alike. Most of them winter in England, and make up for the scarcity of insects by picking bones and eating seeds, for their bills are pretty strong. You can always attract them by hanging up half cocoa-nuts, and as they are useful in the garden and like to nest in holes it is a good plan to fix up a few nesting-boxes for them—with a hole that is big enough for a tit, but too small for a Sparrow. They are fond of deep holes, and you won't get many eggs without that wire scoop I advised you to make. Before they begin to sit they always leave their eggs covered up, as far as I know, so even with the scoop they are not easy to get then. They are good sitters, and hiss and spit at you if you stir them up; but if you retire a little they will generally come out and let you get at the eggs. These are all white with pink spots, and can't be distinguished (except by the size in some cases). They lay a great many, and most of them bring out two broods every summer.

In this family, besides the true Tits, you will find:—

The Bearded Tit, which is not a Tit at all, but nobody seems to know where else to put him;

The Goldcrest, which isn't coloured like a Tit, but acts like one;

The Tree-creeper and Nuthatch, which are really Tits that have taken to Woodpecker habits.

THE LONG-TAILED TIT.

Generally called "Bottle-Tit" in the North.

This, though rare in some parts, is a very well-known bird. You can tell this by the number of names it has, such as "Mum-ruffin," "Oven-bird," "Pudden-bird," and so on. I don't think I need describe it, as it is unmistakable. We have only one smaller bird, the Goldcrest.

Haunts.—You never know where you may come across them in Summer, for they wander about in little parties all Winter, and settle down just where they happen to be when Spring comes round. Their haunts are pretty well anywhere, for woods, gardens, and hedgerows are all much alike to them.

Nesting-place.—I have seen nests against the trunk of a tree, on top of a stump or a big side-branch, in a hedge, a gorse-bush, a bramble bush, to say nothing of hazel, holly, and honeysuckle; so I can't tell you much about where to look.

Nest.—The nest is big and oval, with a hole at the side and quite near the top. It is very cleverly made of lichen, moss and spiders' webs felted together like a Chaffinch's, and well lined with feathers. It matches the grey bark of trees very well, and you might often miss it but for the little round hole; but in other places it shows up rather well. For instance, I once saw one in a gorse-bush at the other side of the road. It didn't look like a nest at all, but I took it for a large lump of cinder or coke, and naturally wanted to know how in the world it had got there, and how it stuck on, too. I don't think the birds ever try to hide their nest, except as you hide the thimble in the well-known game, and if you find one right out of sight, as in a thick hedge, it is just an accident.

Habits.—If you are lucky you may see the bird walk into her nest upside down, loop the loop, and finish up with her nose in the hole and her tail curled over her head, the end perhaps sticking out of the opening.

I have seen two birds come out of the nest one after the other, when there were eggs inside; and some say that the pair of them always sleep in the nest. You may be able to find out if this is true.

Eggs.—The eggs are from six to ten or more, very small and marked with very fine specks, so that they cannot be mixed up with the other Tits'.

Season.—You may find the eggs early in May, but some are much later, and I don't think these are second broods. The time probably depends on when the birds make up their minds to stop wandering and settle down.

2.—THE BLUE TIT.

This is the commonest Tit, and I think the prettiest, and everyone knows him; some are even so familiar as to call him "Jacky Blue-cap."

Haunts.—His haunts are everywhere, and for a nesting place he loves a hole in a wall, but a tree does nearly as well; and there are so many looking out for the same sort of place that he is often driven to find strange quarters, like a letter-box, or a hole in an iron lamp-post. The entrance is nearly always small (or the Sparrows would be there) and the nest often very deep down.

Nest.—It is made mostly of moss, hair, wool and feathers, warm but badly finished. I once knew a Blue Tit to take possession of a nesting-box where a Great Tit had already laid three eggs (and deserted them). She put a very little hair over them and laid nine of her own, which soon settled down among the others, and in the end she hatched the lot. It was very crowded in there, and as the young Great Tits grew up most of the smaller sort got squashed or smothered, till only the three were left. Those three eggs had been ten days in the nest when the Blue Tit began.

Eggs.—They lay a lot of eggs. I believe eighteen is the record, and I have often found 13. You shouldn't leave more than eight or nine in a small hole, or the chicks may die like the little princes in the Tower. They are ordinary Tit eggs, and just like the next two.

Season.—Laying often begins before the end of April, and then you can look for second broods in the same holes in June.

3.—THE COAL TIT.

Bird.—The Coal Tit has a black cap, a white patch at the back of the neck, a grey back, and two bars on the wing.

Haunts.—He is not so common as the Blue Tit, but may be met with anywhere. He uses the same sort of holes, but also likes to nest in a mouse-hole or other hole in the ground. I have known a nest in a hole in a sawn-off tree stump, just a crack in the middle going straight down into the ground—not very comfortable in wet weather, you would think; but a fine lot of young ones came out.

Hints.—Nest and eggs are just like the Blue Tit's, and laying times the same. If you don't see any birds when you find the nest, go back in 2 or 3 weeks, when the young ones will be hatched; you will see the birds coming with food about once a minute, and then you will know.

4.—THE MARSH TIT.

Bird.—He has a black cap like the Coal Tit, but *no white patch* on the nape of the neck. His two white cheek-patches reach round nearly to the back, and you might take them for a white collar, the hair hanging

FIG. 15—NIGHTJAR
(see page 127)

FIG. 16—NIGHTJAR (sitting)

(see page 127)

over it at the back. His back is grey-brown, and his wings have no bars, so you ought to be able to recognize him.

Haunts.—He is rarer than the Coal Tit, so is worth looking out for. His haunts are not marshy any more than the other Tits', and you may find him anywhere, even in your own garden.

Nesting-place.—He likes a hole that is low down, and often chooses a rotten stump or gatepost, in which he digs one for himself; so look out for chips if you see one about.

Otherwise he is just like the other Tits in his habits, nest, eggs and season.

5.—THE GREAT TIT.
" Ox-eye " or " Saw-sharpener."

Bird.—The first name he gets from his white cheek-patches, and his other points are: black head, greenish back, one bar on the wing, and yellow breast with a thick black line down the middle, which broadens out into a black patch on the belly (you can tell him by this even when he is up above with his tail towards you).

The second name tells you the sort of noise he makes when he thinks he is singing. I have already warned you not to mistake it for the Chiff-Chaff's effort. Besides this he makes most of the usual Tit noises, and his wife spits and hisses like the rest of them when you venture to look into the nest.

The Great Tit is often quite as common as the Blue, and his places and times are the same as the others, but his eggs you can tell because they are bigger.

Habits.—One difference is that while a Blue Tit, for instance, thinks nothing of flying into her nest while you are walking past or standing close by, Great Tits are very shy of giving their nest away, and I have found far more of them by poking about in holes than by watching the birds.

6.—THE CRESTED TIT.

This is one of the rarest British birds, I think only found in the valley of the Spey in Scotland. If you are there and see a brownish-looking Tit with a whitish crest, that will be it. It lives in fir woods chiefly, and is said to like to dig its own hole, and the eggs are a little bigger than the smaller Tits', and less than the Great Tits'. Everything else is just like the rest of the family. The birds' crests are unmistakable, consisting of long black feathers with white tips.

7.—THE BEARDED TIT.

This is another very rare bird, only found on the Norfolk Broads, and not common there.

It is not a Tit at all, but a little bird with a very long tail, and the cock has a blue head and black moustache to distinguish him from the hen, who is just a sort of tawny colour, lighter below. They fly like Wagtails, and have a call which sounds like "ping-ping."

They haunt reed-beds, and there may be a few in other places than the Broads, but I doubt it.

The nest is on the ground or nearly so, among the sedge; the six eggs are white, marked with short thin *lines* of dark brown, and there are two broods, starting perhaps before the end of April.

8.—THE GOLDCREST (Fig. 13).

Bird.—This is not only the smallest British bird, but the smallest in Europe; but he is pretty hardy, and a lot of them spend the Winter here. You have to be pretty near one to see his yellow crest and barred wings. He is greenish above and buff below, but for all that you can know him for a Tit up in the tree-tops by his way of running up one twig and fluttering to the next. He is very tame, and if you see one in a hedge you can go within six feet without scaring him. If you know his high squeaky note very like a mouse's you can generally tell when you are near a nest. He also sings a cheery little song, pitched in the same high key.

Haunts.—His haunts are fir woods, which need not be big; in fact he will nest anywhere where there are fir trees, and in my experience prefers young ones, say 20 to 30 feet high.

Nest.—I have never seen a nest higher than 20 feet up, but they may easily be much higher (and pretty safe not to be found). A good number can be reached from the ground, and I have seen one no higher than 3 feet.

The nest is a fine work of art, equal to the Chaffinch or Long-tailed Tit's. It is a tiny round cup slung underneath the branch, generally near the end, by the twigs being bent down and woven into the nest, or occasionally by little ropes of cobweb and moss. It is chiefly made of these two things, woven into a thick felt, and is lined with plenty of feathers.

The nest is hard to see even when it is just above you, and generally takes some finding; and though the bird sits close when she is on, you will not see either of them much about the neighbourhood of the nest. Their call-note is the best guide as to where to look, if you can hear it. The cock sings, but not always near the nest.

Eggs.—The eggs are six or eight, very pale brown with a few dark-red specks, or none at all. They are so small that there can be no mistake about who laid them.

Season.—They often lay by the end of April, but early May is the best time, and some are later. I have never known of a second brood.

9.—THE TREE-CREEPER.

Bird.—This is a little mouse-coloured bird, with a speckled back and white breast, which you will see running up the tree trunks just like a mouse. His outline from the side is like a bended bow, from the tip of his long curved bill to the points of his stiff curved tail-feathers, which grip the bark and help to keep him in position.

Haunts.—You may see them all through the Winter, searching the crevices of the bark for a stray spider or insect, and not always in the woods, which are their chief nesting place. Big old trees are what they want, and they may choose one in an orchard, or right away from other trees if it is the right sort. A great many of the nests you will find will be near water of some kind, but I cannot say why.

Nest.—The nest is either built in a narrow hole or crack in the tree itself, or just wedged in behind a piece of loose bark or ivy that has partly come away. It is easily recognized, for it is built of small twigs and chips of wood, with a good soft lining, generally of feathers. Sometimes a crack is filled up with twigs for quite a long way, till it gets wide enough for the nest (but it need not be much wider than an inch and a half).

The only times you will see a Tree-creeper sitting still are, first when she is on her nest, and then when you have frightened her off, when she may sit close by, perhaps on the trunk of the next tree, till you go away.

Eggs.—The eggs are just the same as the Tits', but you can judge by the nest even if the bird is not about.

Season.—Early May, if not before; and there is often a second brood in June.

10.—THE NUTHATCH.

Bird.—This is a bigger bird, slate-grey on the back and orange in front, and runs up trees in the same way.

Haunts.—It does not come further North than South Yorkshire, and hardly migrates at all, so that there is very little chance of meeting it in the North.

Nest.—Its haunts are woods, and its nest is very peculiar. It chooses a hole in a tree, and whatever size it may be, plasters it up with mud, leaving a round hole just big enough to get in and out by. This mud is often grooved so that it looks just like the bark, and I have mistaken one for a Woodpecker's hole and not discovered my mistake till I got right up to it. The nest itself is just a few dead leaves and chips of wood at the bottom of the hole.

Eggs.—The usual number of eggs is seven, of the family colour, but rather bigger than a Great Tit's.

THE CLIMBERS.

That is the end of the Perchers, and you will notice that the last two, though their feet are meant for perching, have taken to climbing. The real climbing birds have two toes pointing forward and two backward, and we have not many of them. Four Woodpeckers and the Cuckoo are the only birds with the proper sort of feet, and the last does not climb. There are three other birds that are related to them, but they have very little right to be called Climbers. The Kingfisher comes in here because he is very like a Woodpecker in beak and build, and the Swift and Nightjar are sort of waifs and strays. You might almost say they had been adopted by the Climbers because no one else would have them.

FAMILY XIII.—THE WOODPECKERS.

These birds are so much alike that I will take them all together. Besides their feet, which you know about, their chief points are big strong beaks, bright colours, stiff tails for steadying them against the tree, and loud ringing cries. They generally dig out holes for themselves, which are round, and go straight in for a few inches, and then turn down for a foot or less, when they widen out into the nest-chamber. There is no nest but the chips of wood, and the eggs are from 5 to 8, pure white and very polished. They hatch in about a fortnight, the young ones come out blind, naked and helpless, and they grow no down, but stay naked till the feathers come. There is no second brood. Now I will take them separately.

I.—THE GREATER SPOTTED WOODPECKER
(Fig. 14).

Bird.—Black and white, barred rather than spotted, and about as big as a Starling. Has a loud cry and a trick of rattling on a branch with his bill, which you should hear, as he is the only one that lives in the North, the others all being purely South-country birds.

Haunts.—Big woods, often of fir trees; but for his nest he chooses a birch or something like that, often a rotten old stump, and that makes it easier to find, where most of the timber is fir.

Season.—Early June is the usual time, though it will be as well to look for eggs before that, as the birds are generally here all the Winter.

2.—THE LESSER SPOTTED WOODPECKER.

Bird.—Like the last, but about as big as a Sparrow.

Haunts.—Never very common, and doesn't come North of Yorkshire. Nests in woods, orchards and hedgerow trees, sometimes making its hole in the trunk, sometimes in a branch quite high up. Laying begins early in May in the South, and this bird is there all Winter, too.

3.—THE GREEN WOODPECKER.

Bird.—As big as a Missel Thrush, and flies like one. Colour green, yellow on the rump, with a bright red crest on its head. Rare in Yorkshire, but pretty common further South.

Haunts.—Generally makes its hole in a sound tree (outside at any rate), and likes open woods and clumps of trees. Often lays before the end of April.

Cry.—Can easily be known by its loud, laughing cry, and is often called the " Yaffil " accordingly.

4.—THE WRYNECK.

Bird.—Very unlike the others. Mottled brown like a Woodcock, with a broad tail with three bars across it; breast yellowish, with black bars. His cry is sharp, and sounds like " qui qui qui."

Haunts.—He is a rare bird, not to be found except here and there in the South and East. He sticks to the woods, and is more often heard than seen. Having not nearly such a strong beak as the real Woodpeckers, he uses a readymade hole.

Season.—The eggs are not laid much before June, for this bird is a migrant, and comes in April. The eggs come between the Greater and Lesser Spotted Woodpeckers in size.

FAMILY XIV.—THE CUCKOO.

(Often called the " Gowk " in the North.)

Bird.—His head, neck and upper parts are blue-grey, and his breast barred like a Sparrow Hawk's, and both his shape and his way of flying are a very good imitation of a Hawk, but his feet are like a Woodpecker's, and his bill only fit for catching insects.

Calls.—Everyone knows the cock Cuckoo's call, but the hen has a different note altogether, a loud shrill ringing " pip-pip-pip-pip . . . ." not unlike the twitter of a Dabchick or the scream of a Hawk; and when you hear this coming from a wood or clump of trees you will know that that is her headquarters, and may expect to find her eggs in any of the small nests round about. You may hear cockbirds calling all over the place, but you have small hopes of finding an egg unless you are near the hen bird's haunt.

Haunts.—The first week in May is the Cuckoo's time for arriving in the North, and you don't need to see him to know he is here. His haunts may be almost anywhere, but up here I think you see most Cuckoos on the edge of the moor, where the Meadow Pipits are.

CUCKOO. 121

Nests.—Everyone knows that a Cuckoo leaves the hatching part to some other bird, and a Meadow Pipit is about her first choice. In the North the next best are Tree Pipits, Hedge Sparrows and Wagtails. Warblers will do, too, and where Reed Warblers are common they get a lot of her custom.

Eggs.—A Cockoo's egg is about the size of a Sparrow's, and with such a small egg goes the instinct to put it in a small nest; each Cuckoo is sure to try and find a nest like the one it was brought up in, *and* the odd ones that one hears of in a Grebe's nest or a Jay's wouldn't keep up *that* custom, for they wouldn't be brought up at all! So you need not expect to find Cuckoos' eggs in big birds' nests.

They are supposed to be all sorts of colours from speckled brown to plain blue, and to be sometimes, but not always, placed in nests with eggs of the same colour.

Your trouble is that short of seeing the Cuckoo lay her egg in the nest you can never be sure of your egg unless it *is* different in colour. For every bird from a Golden Eagle to a Goldcrest is liable to lay one egg rather larger or a lot smaller than the rest; but you do not find a bird getting a different shade of paint on one of her eggs—thicker or thinner it may be, and generally thinnest on the extra big egg. So a speckled egg in a Hedge Sparrow's nest is pretty sure to be a Cuckoo's, but a big blue one is just as likely to be a double-yolked Hedge Sparrow's. There is only one way to make certain of that egg, and unless you only collect eggs with a camera, as I do, I know you won't do it. For it is to leave it there and *see what comes out.*

Young.—A very young Cuckoo has a hollow in his back. As he snuggles down into the nest, the eggs or young birds roll into this hollow. Not liking the weight on his back, he hoists himself up, and quite unconsciously tips the unfortunate thing out of the nest. This goes on till he has the place to himself, as a rule, and as he gets older the hollow fills up. (The birds never seem to notice the murders, either because they can't count or because their big chick keeps them too busy feeding him.) Now I think this hollow arrangement is one of the most wonderful things in Nature. What do you think? You think you'll wait till you see it? Quite right; and I hope you see it this season.

Season.—You won't find an egg much before June 1st.

FAMILY XV.
THE KINGFISHERS.

Again we have only one of them, and not nearly as many of him as their ought to be.

Most of the Kingfisher family are tropical birds, and that accounts for our bird's brilliant plumage.

Bird.—His back is the brightest blue you will see on any bird, and his breast orange. He has a short tail and a beak like a spear-head, and flies fast and straight as an arrow over the water. He has a shrill, sharp call-note, which you don't hear very often, but which you can't mistake once you know it.

Habits.—Though he belongs to a tropical family, he manages to stick out the English winter, and you generally see the old birds haunting the place where the nest was, though the young ones clear off as soon as they are old enough, and precious few of them come back in Spring.

His way of fishing is to sit still on a branch or post till a minnow swims within range, when he dives like an arrow and generally comes up with it. Then he flies back to his perch like a Flycatcher, knocks it on the head and swallows it, and is ready for the next. Watch him if you get the chance; it is worth it.

Haunts.—The Kingfisher is not like the Dipper, but likes slow-running streams, and the place to find one is any part of a brook or river where there are steep earth banks. I have seen him amongst Sand Martins, but I think he favours good stiff clay, and his Woodpecker beak can pick a hole almost anywhere.

Nest.—His nest is at the end of a long tunnel, which is generally oval, but higher than it is broad, never flattened like a Sand Martin's. It is almost always near the top of the bank, and slopes slightly up to the nest, for drainage.

The nest is nothing but fish-bones and scales, which he does not digest but throws up again, and on these the eggs lie.

Eggs.—The eggs may be as many as eight, pure white and very glossy, and almost round, like a Woodpecker's in fact.

Season.—The season for laying varies rather, but I have generally found eggs about the middle of May.

Hints.—Suppose you come across a Kingfisher, the first thing is to find the right hole, for there may be several that look like it.

Signs.—The hole is often where some ends of roots stick out from the bank, and if so the birds will perch on them, and you are sure to see a few white droppings on or under them. Another sign to look for is a little heap of white fish scales and bones at the foot of the bank. That is a sign of spring-cleaning, for when the birds come back to the old hole (as they generally do) they throw out last year's rubbish, and it lies where it fell, and tells you where their hole is. The next move is to put your nose to the hole, and if you smell fish, and *not* damp earth, there is a pretty good chance that the eggs are laid.

Next get a good long stick and poke it carefully right to the end; if you keep it pressed against the *top* there is no fear of breaking the eggs, and if the bird is at home she comes out soon after the stick is withdrawn, and you are sure it is all right, for you don't want to interfere with the nest before there are eggs in it.

Now to get at the nest. If it goes under a big tree root you can't do it; but if the ground on top is clear you can. But you will need a spade, this trick is hard to do with a trowel.

Measuring.—First measure the hole very carefully with your stick, and mark on the top the place where the nest should be. This is hard to do, but if you do it three times and it comes within an inch or two you've probably got it.

Digging.—Now dig a trench, leading up to the nest from the back, but stopping a foot short of it, and make the end next the nest a good deal deeper than what you think is the level of the nest. Now all you have to do is to keep a straight face on this end of your trench and advance it slowly, like a sap, tapping the face as you go, till at last you hear a hollow sound and can tell just where the nest is. Now work carefully till the wall is quite thin, cut a piece out with your knife, and you can examine the nest and get an egg out without disturbing it at all.

Filling Up.—Put a good stiff slab of clay firmly over your private entrance, fill up the trench, put the sods back carefully on top, scatter the surplus earth, and no one, perhaps not even the bird herself, can tell you have been there.

Caution.—Make your trench big enough to start with, so that you can work comfortably at the forward end. It needs to be wide to allow for a mistake in the measuring, too, and you will not often find the nest turn up right in the middle of your working face, however careful you are. You don't want to spoil a Kingfisher's nest, for they are far too rare as it is.

If you find one you can't get at, let it alone; but if you plug it well up in the Autumn the birds may dig a new one next year, and in a better place.

FAMILY XVI.
SWIFTS AND NIGHTJARS.

We may as well take the waifs together, and they have a good deal in common in their inside arrangements, though all you can see outside is:—

First, they both pretend to be someone else; one looks like a Swallow, the other like a Hawk.

Second, they both catch insects on the wing, and have a wide mouth for doing it.

Third, they both lay two long-shaped eggs.

Fourth, they are both migrants that come very late.

I.—THE SWIFT.
Or " Black Martin."

Bird.—This bird looks like one of the Swallows, and has longer wings than any of them; it is rusty black all over except for a white throat. It gives a piercing scream when flying, and it is hardly ever seen on the ground. Indeed some say it cannot rise if it once settles, as its feet are so feeble that it can't jump high enough to get its long wings spread. All its toes are turned forward, so that perching is out of the question, but it *can* cling to its nest-hole, though you will generally see it shut its wings and dive straight in.

Haunts.—It is not a very common bird, but most villages and towns have a few, which fly about together as a rule, and there are often little colonies in cliffs, ruined castles and abbeys, and such places.

Nest.—It nests in narrow holes in cliffs, and often in a cleft under the eaves of a house; but church towers are perhaps its favourite haunt. The nest is made of straw and feathers, glued together with some sticky stuff from the bird's mouth. The bird's nest soup that the Chinese are so fond of is made from the nests of another kind of Swift.

Eggs.—The two eggs are white, rough-shelled, and very long in shape.

Season.—The birds don't arrive till May, and will not have eggs before June.

Note.—The Swift is the fastest bird that flies, and its wings never seem to tire. Some believe that it *sleeps* on the wing, as an Albatross is supposed to do. At any rate it is quite a common thing for the birds to fly about all day, and then at dusk to start racing madly about over the house-tops and through the streets, screaming as they go. Soon they begin to mount higher and higher, till they go clean out of sight, and you may sit up and watch all night, but you never see or hear them coming back; and all next day they are flying about as usual.

2.—THE NIGHTJAR (Figs. 15, 16).
" Fern Owl " or " Goat-sucker."

Bird.—This is a brown-mottled bird with a long tail, which looks very like a small Hawk when flying. Its note is " chur-r-r-r-," going on like a rattle for minutes at a time, and never heard till it is almost dark. The birds also have a note like " chuck, chuck," and clap their wings over their backs with a sharp click when flying.

The cock has white ticks on his wings and tail, but the hen is all brown, and this is important to know, for if a *hen* rises from a certain spot in the day-time, *that* is where she will lay her eggs later on, if they are not there already.

They fly about at night, catching moths and beetles, and often sing (or rather rattle) sitting *lengthways* on a branch—so if they are not much like Climbers, they are still less like Perchers.

Haunts.—Its favourite haunts are bracken-covered places with trees about, and open spaces among woods, but it often nests on the open moor, with no trees near.

Nest.—It nests in fern or heather, laying its two eggs on some little patch of bare peat as a rule. The bird sits closely and is very hard to see, but will get up if your feet or stick come really near. Remember again that even if there are no eggs where a hen bird rises, she is almost certain to lay on that very spot.

Eggs.—The two eggs are long-shaped, with both ends alike, and are mottled and veined all over with about three shades of brown and grey. You can't mistake them.

Season.—This is the latest of all the migrants, and the time for eggs is not before the middle of June, and may be well into July. I have seen downy young ones on the 12th of August.

THE BIRDS OF PREY.

This group have feet like the Perching birds, but all have long hooked claws with which they strike and carry their prey, and strong hooked beaks for eating it. They like to kill their own meat, and eat it fresh and warm.

Three of the five families make good big nests, and the other two have no idea of making a nest at all.

Their eggs are either plain white or marked with red blotches which fade to brown, like blood-stains. They take longer to hatch than any we have had so far (four weeks on the average), and the young ones are about a week older when they come out, fairly active and covered with white down, instead of helpless and naked.

FAMILY XVII.
THE EAGLES.

Most of this family will not come your way, for the few that are left are pretty well looked after; though you may be taken to *see* a nest under escort. In that case you will have someone to tell you all about it. So I will just say a very little about the first three.

1. The Golden Eagle only nests in the Highlands and Islands now, and lays in March or early in April.

2. The White-tailed Eagle is even rarer, and found chiefly on the West coast of Scotland, and nests about the same time.

FIG. 17—BUZZARD
(see page 129)

FIG. 18 SPARROW HAWK
(see page 131)

3. The Kite is very nearly extinct in Britain, and one place where there used to be a nest in Wales had to have regular sentries to keep egg-collectors away. You can always tell a Kite by its forked tail, and it builds its nest in a tree and lays in May.

4.—THE BUZZARD (Fig. 17).

Bird.—This is a big brown bird, with a habit of soaring round and round up aloft and making a noise like a cat mewing.

Haunts and Nest.—They are not very rare in the Lake District and I have seen them in North Wales. They build a big nest of sticks among the crags, often inaccessible but sometimes quite easy to get at.

The nest is lined with twigs with green leaves on them.

Eggs.—The eggs are two or three, white with red or rusty markings, and bigger than any other Hawk's you will find.

Season.—They are laid in April or May, and the nest is not ready till it has the green leaves in it.

FAMILY XVIII.
THE HAWKS.

These are a rather smaller lot, and can be distinguished from the Falcons, the next family, by having a longer tail and shorter wings, and a different way of hunting. They also have yellow eyes, and the true Falcons' are almost black. There is only one you are likely to get, but I will mention them all.

I. The Goshawk used to be a favourite in the old days of Falconry, and perhaps used to breed in England, but certainly has not for many years.

The **Harriers** are going the same road, but there is always a chance of meeting one of them. They are big hawks which hunt over open ground, beating slowly up against the wind, like a pointer or setter, and then sailing back down wind for another beat. You can recognize a Harrier by this way of hunting, and now I will describe the different kinds, and where they are to be met with.

Birds and Haunts.

2. Montagu's Harrier is a Fen bird, and nests fairly often in Wicken Fen, the only place in England where I have seen it. The cock is slaty blue and the hen brown.

3. The Hen Harrier is a moor bird, and still to be found occasionally in the West. The cock is slate-blue with a white rump, the hen brown, also with a white rump and five distinct dark bars on the tail.

4. The Marsh Harrier was another bird of the Fens, now nearly extinct. The cock bird is brown and silver-grey above, and the hen browner.

If you get a chance at any of these birds, be careful to watch the hen. The cock is more likely to lead you to Ducks' and other birds' nests, than to his own; but you might see him come along with some food for his mate, who will rise from the nest to take it.

Nests.—All these birds nest on the ground, and make pretty good nests of whatever is handy—twigs, reeds, sedge, heather and so on.

Eggs.—They all lay from four to six eggs, bluish white with no markings, or hardly any.

Season.—Late May or early June is the time.

Caution.—If you find one, take an egg or a photograph, but give the birds a chance and *don't tell anyone else.*

5.—THE SPARROW HAWK (Fig. 18).

Bird.—The cock has a blue back and barred breast, like a Cuckoo. The hen has a brown back and is nearly twice his size, as with most Hawks. They hunt small birds along the hedges, flying low and coming suddenly on them over the top or round a corner. They have a shrill scream, which you soon get to know, but which is just like the cries of the small Falcons.

Haunts and Nest.—Sparrow Hawks always nest in woods, and like the rest of this family build their own nest; at least I only remember one pair that did not, and they used the old Carrion Crow's nest that you have heard of already.

The nest is generally high up, but not always, and in some sort of a fir tree for choice. It may be next the trunk, or right out along a branch, and I think the birds like a place from which they have a good view, though I *have* found nests in very thick parts of a wood.

It is a broad, flat nest made of twigs, with a slight hollow for the eggs, and takes a long time to finish, and when it *is* finished they generally wait a week or so before beginning to lay. It is generally easy to see from the ground, and especially when there are young ones there will be a lot of white down sticking about the nest and the branches near it.

Eggs.—The eggs are from 4 to 6, ground colour white, with a blue tint in it, and markings big blotches of red-brown, generally dark but sometimes very pale, and a well-marked Sparrow Hawk's egg is one of the handsomest there is.

Season.—They *may* lay in April, but I have seldom found them before the second half of May.

FAMILY XIX.
THE FALCONS.

The Falcons have long pointed wings, breasts generally streaked, not barred (though an old Peregrine has short bars on his), and black eyes. Their way of hunting is to climb up in circles above their prey and come down on it with a rush, " stooping " it is called. They have no idea of making a nest, but lay their eggs in holes in the rocks or in other birds' nests, such as Crows' or Magpies'. The eggs are mottled all over with red—brick-red when fresh-laid, but soon turning brown.

1—THE PEREGRINE FALCON (Fig. 19).

This is a big bird that flies at Grouse, Ducks, Pigeons and birds of that size, and is the favourite bird with the few people who still go in for Falconry.

A few pairs still nest in the crags of the Lake District and other high mountains, and on rocky parts of the coast, and if you *should* get a chance at one, you should find eggs by the middle of May. There are sometimes four, but more often three, though I once found five.

2.—THE MERLIN.
" Blue Hawk " or " Rock Kestrel."

Bird.—His names don't describe him very well, for it is only an old cock that is blue on the back, and they do not often nest in rocks. Most Merlins are a sober brown colour, and their breasts well streaked with dark brown.

He flies at Larks, Wheatears and other small birds, and is as good a flier as the Peregrine, or better, for a Lark is difficult game. I have seen both Hawk and Lark mount clean out of sight, and once I saw a Merlin, after missing a Lark a dozen times, turn sharp in his dive and shoot straight up again, catching the Lark quite unawares in his upward rush. I hope you may see two Merlins playing together in the air, and you will see one of the prettiest sights there are, *and* some of the trickiest flying imaginable. If you feel tempted to go in for Falconry, a young Merlin is the bird to start on, and you will find all you want to know about it in the Badminton Library.

Haunts and Nest.—Heather moors are where Merlins breed, and I can't give you much help in finding their nests, for they just use a hollow in the heather, which is sometimes on a steep slope and sometimes on the level, even on an open flowe or moss much as Dunlins like. The bird doesn't wait to be trodden on, but gets up at a reasonable distance, so that you must mark the spot well if you are to find the nest. If you find one you are very likely to find it about the same spot next year.

Eggs.—Four or five, Falcon colour. You can't distinguish them from a Kestrel's.

Season.—They should be sitting by the first week in June, and that is the best time for finding them. Merlins go away for the winter, but not very far, as there are plenty in Ireland or along our South coast then.

3.—THE HOBBY.

Bird.—This bird has a back like a Merlin's, but a yellow breast with distinct black markings, short streaks or long spots.

Habits.—It is a Summer bird, and very few ever get as far as Yorkshire, and even in the South it is rare. It flies at small birds like the Merlin, and is said to be able to catch Swallows, and like most little Hawks, does not despise good big beetles, the hard parts of which you will find in all their castings.

Haunts, Etc.—It likes big woods in the lowlands, just the opposite of the Merlin's haunts, and uses an old nest of a Magpie or other bird, where it generally lays three eggs, of the usual colour, early in June as a rule.

4.—THE KESTREL.
Or "Windhover."

Bird.—This is the commonest Falcon, bright red-brown on the back, breast yellowish and lightly streaked with dark brown. The cock in full plumage has a blue head and tail.

Hovering.—This Falcon flies at *mice*, and so has no need to climb above his prey in rings; he hovers instead, head to wind, with his wings just quivering to keep him there, watching to see a mouse move in the grass. When he sees one, he drops like a stone and turns within an inch of the ground, shooting out his claws and seizing the mouse as he does so. You will not see any other bird hover as a Kestrel does—the others do it head up and tail down, and wings beating hard.

Haunts.—They nest either in cliffs or woods. Only where there are neither, as in the Fens, will you find them using a nest in a single tree, and there the Magpies and Carrion Crows are doing the same.

Nest.—They generally choose a nest of one of those two birds, and make no alterations. They may scratch the root lining out of a Magpie's to make more room, but I have found their eggs in good new Magpies' nests where they hadn't done so. In a hole in a cliff the eggs are laid on the bare rock, and if there are a few castings to make the floor softer, I think it is just untidiness on the bird's part.

Kestrels are pretty quick to leave their nests, so if you want to find where they are in a cliff you should sneak up very carefully to some spot where you have a good view, and then clap your hands, when you are pretty sure to see them come out. On a wet day you may see one get off a nest in a tree, but it is generally a case of climb up and try your luck.

Eggs.—The four to seven eggs are just like the other small Falcons', but some show a little of the white ground-colour.

Season.—Early May is not too soon for a Kestrel.

FAMILY XX.
THE OSPREY.

This is a big Hawk with very long wings, and extra long claws for seizing his prey, which is fish; they are almost like hooks, but he has not managed to grow barbs on them yet. These birds only nest in one or two places in Scotland, where they are protected. They build enormous nests, on a tree-top or on an old ruin, and their eggs are the finest of the lot, richly marked like a Sparrow Hawk's and as big as a Buzzard's—but they are not for you, unless you try America, where they are quite common.

FAMILY XXI.
THE OWLS. (" HOOLETS.")

Everyone knows the wise look of an Owl, and how different it is from all other birds, but not everyone has considered why it is so different. All other birds have an eye at each side, so that they can keep a look out for danger on both sides at once. An owl has nothing to be afraid of, and has to see in the dark, so he has his eyes both in front, where they can work together like yours or mine. He also has them enormously big, for they have to be very sensitive, and his ears have to be big, too, to catch any little rustle that a mouse makes; so now you see that his big head is not all brains. If you have ears that can hear a mouse's footstep they are not much good unless you go softly yourself, so we find that an owl's feathers are so broad and soft that he can slip along without a sound. I remember one taking my cap off as I was coming down from her nest. I felt a bang on the head and saw the owl slide away with my cap in her claws, but I never heard the faintest sound before or after, and that was in broad daylight when owls are supposed to be half blind and clumsy.

Most owls have feathers on their feet, but whether that helps them in their trade I don't know. The only other things I have to say about Owls are that none of them know how to make a nest, and they all lay pure white eggs.

I.—THE BARN OWL (Fig. 20).

Bird.—This is not a common bird, but if you see one you will not mistake it for any other owl, as it is nearly all white on the face and breast.

Haunts.—It may haunt a barn, but more often chooses a church tower, or some kind of ruin. It is said to nest in a hole in a tree sometimes.

Eggs.—The eggs are from four to six, about as big as a Woodpigeon's, and laid in the hole where it rests during the day. That is probably why young owls are often at different ages, as the bird has nowhere else to go and starts hatching them by mistake as it were. The eggs are not laid every day, but at intervals of a few days as a rule, which makes the difference in ages bigger.

Season.—The first eggs are laid about April, but if you should only find the nest by seeing the Owls feeding their young ones, you may find another lot of eggs later on, for they often have several broods, and eggs have been found as late as October. These Owls do not migrate, and where they have snug quarters and a good supply of mice, they could bring up a family all right in December.

2.—THE BROWN OWL (Fig. 21).

Wood Owl, Tawny Owl or Screech Owl.

Bird.—This is the biggest of all, and can be recognized on the wing by its big head, which looks as if it had been cut square across in front. It is the only one that really hoots, and has a variety of weird screeches as well.

Haunts and Nesting-places.—It is the commonest Owl where there are big old trees, for it loves a hole in a tree, and though it is called the Wood Owl I have found lots of them nesting in suitable holes far enough from the nearest wood. If holes are scarce the unlucky ones use old nests of Magpies, etc., and I have found several using Squirrels'. And now and then they lay on the ground under a thick spreading fir, in the space between two roots, which I suppose feels something like a hole; it is dark anyhow. I once climbed up an eight foot stump to see if there was a hole in the top, and found it was nothing *but* hole, and there was a Brown Owl sitting on her eggs at the bottom. I took her for a rabbit till she moved, and when she did she flew up and out in a little less time than it took me to get my face out of the way. I did some fishing before I got one of those eggs out.

Eggs.—Two eggs are not uncommon, three the regular thing, and four the most I have seen. They are too big to be taken for any other Owl's. The family often come on in instalments, as Barn Owls do.

Season.—The first eggs may be found as early as the end of March, and there is often a second brood or even a third perhaps, though not in my experience.

3.—THE LONG-EARED OWL.

Bird.—More often called Horned Owl, or just "Hornie," and the tufts of feathers in question are nowhere near his *ears*, but very like horns indeed. He is a slim-looking Owl with the usual streaky plumage, and when he perches in his usual day-time place, leaning his head against the tree-trunk like some reveller against a lamp-post, he is quite hard to see. His cry is like a Peewit's.

Haunts and Nests.—He is the commonest Owl where big old trees are scarce, and where all the woods are larch and fir plantations, often the only Owl you will see. He never uses holes to my knowledge, but always takes a second-hand nest, a Magpie's for choice, and 1 have known him use one in a thorn-bush on the moor, which I could reach from the ground.

Habits.—Some sit very tight, and will only cluck and snore at you if you poke them, and I once took an egg from under one like a pickpocket, and left her sitting; but nine out of ten will fly off if you tap the tree.

Eggs.—The eggs are generally four, and you can't tell them from a Woodpigeon's or a Barn Owl's. But there is not much fear of you mixing them up with either. If you should find three eggs on a Woodpigeon's nest, and no bird on, it will be interesting, and you have got something good whichever they turn out to be.

Season.—The first week of April or earlier is the time, and I have never found a second brood.

Note.—I once found a Sparrow Hawk's nest building, unmistakable, though I never saw the bird at it. When I thought it would be finished I went again and found a Horned Owl with three eggs in it, *and* the nest properly finished, so I had no choice but to believe that she did it herself. But as that was 23 years ago, and I have never seen anything like it since, I think now that the Owl had just come along and taken a fancy to the nest while the Hawk was away (you know they don't begin to lay for a week or so after the nest is finished). No other Owl I have ever known has had any notion of nest-building at all, so I expect that is what happened.

4.—THE SHORT-EARED OWL.

Or " Woodcock Owl."

Bird.—Not unlike the last bird, but a *little* smaller. You don't see the short " ears " as a rule, for it lives in the open and flies about in the daytime like a Hawk, and if you see one doing this on the moors or marshes it is pretty sure to be this Owl. Its cry is very like a Peewit's.

Haunts.—It is a very rare bird in the North and not common anywhere. I have only seen it nesting among sedge, in the Fens, but if you find one in the North it is more likely to be on the heather.

This is one of the Owls that migrate, and in certain years when there was a plague of field-mice, they came over here in swarms, and had a good time. They are said to have laid about twice as many eggs as usual, as there was plenty to feed large families, and that is a wonderful thing and takes some explaining, but not so wonderful as how they got to know about the mice.

Nest.—The eggs are laid in a hollow in the ground, often not hidden at all, a funny predicament for pure white eggs. The bird sits pretty closely, so there is no difficulty in finding them if you flush her. But lots of people seeing an *Owl* rise from the heather or beside a whin-bush would never think of looking for a nest at all.

Eggs.—There may be as many as seven, and they are *creamy* white, like a Stockdove's. Apart from that you can't mistake them, for no other Owl would think of laying in such a place.

Season.—May is the time for eggs, and there is no second brood as a rule, though they are said to have reared several during the plague of mice.

5.—THE LITTLE OWL.

Not much bigger than a Thrush, so you can't mistake it. It has a sort of Peewit cry, and goes " flip flop " with its wings when it rises, like a Woodcock, It was introduced some years back and has spread all over the Eastern counties, at least as far as the Trent valley, so we shall most likely have a few in the North before long. I don't know very much about their habits, but the only two nests I have seen were in holes in pollard willows, and had three eggs and five, early in

May. It does not seem to migrate regularly, so it probably nests a good deal earlier at times, and from the way it has increased in a few years I should say it must have more than one brood.

Note.

On the " Castings " of Birds of Prey.

Owls and Hawks feed ravenously, and swallow fur, feathers, bones, beak and claws all at once. The only trace of a Sparrow Hawk's meal as a rule is a little ring of feathers round the spot where he has been eating. But these indigestible parts get no further than the bird's crop, and he spits them out again in little pellets called " castings."

A few of these on the ground under a nest or hole give you a useful hint, but a great many generally mean you are under the place where an Owl rests in the daytime, and if you go up to the nest you are more likely to find a half-eaten mouse than eggs.

You can tell a Brown Owl's castings from a Horned Owl's, they are much broader and bigger, and it is quite interesting to pull them to pieces and see what the bird has been feeding on. Beetles' wing cases and Grasshoppers' legs generally mean a Kestrel, if the rest is mouse-fur; feathers mean a Sparrow-Hawk as a rule, or a Merlin if you find them out on the open moor.

Other birds throw up castings as well, if they swallow anything they can't digest. Thus Kingfishers throw up fish bones, Rooks, the husks of corn, and Black-backed Gulls, bones and feathers, etc., when they have been having a meal of that sort. I don't know whether Nightjars do or not, but probably not, as they have their crop below their breast-bone.

FAMILY XXII.
THE PIGEONS.

This is the last family of what I call the Tree Birds, and very different from the rest of them. They perch, but their feet are not a bit like the "Perchers," neither are their bills, and their nearest relations are the next family, the Game-birds, which are ground birds, and scratch for their food.

Blue is the usual colour among pigeons, and they mostly have reddish legs and feet. They are strong fliers and easy to recognize on the wing, for they keep their wings going the whole time. At mating time they have a curious trick of soaring over their nesting-place which you are sure to notice, and the cock-birds all go through some kind of performance like what you see tame pigeons doing on the roof, puffing out their crops, spreading their tails, and doing a sort of shuffling dance. Their note is always some sort of " coo," and they build flat nests of twigs and lay only two eggs at a time (always white), and have several broods to make up for this. The young ones when hatched are downy, but pretty helpless, and at first are fed on " pigeons' milk," which I think is the juice of the corn in the old one's crop. The young one sticks its bill right down the old one's throat and sucks it up.

Young Pigeons stay a long time in the nest, often after they seem to be quite full-grown.

I.—THE WOODPIGEON.
" Cushat " in the North, and " Ring Dove " in some books.

Bird.—This is the commonest of the lot, both in Summer and Winter, and you can recognize him by the white " ring," which only goes round the sides of his neck, not back and front, by the broad white bars on his wings as he flies, and by his size, for he is the biggest. His " coo " is rather peculiar, what is called in Greek verse an Anapaest, or in Morse · — — · — which you will most likely understand better.

Haunts.—Thick fir-woods are its favourite haunt, and close to the trunk of a spruce is the favourite place for the nest; but I have found them in all sorts of trees, or among ivy, in tall hawthorn bushes in a hedge or elsewhere, and even in a cypress in a garden.

Nest.—The nest is just twigs laid flat one across the other, and you can often see daylight through it, and sometimes even the eggs. I think they build on more as the twins grow up, but that you can easily find out; anyhow all *old* nests seem to be pretty thick and solid. Sometimes they use an old nest, or build a new one on top, but I think not very often, to judge by the number of nests you see in any thick wood; you will often see a bird get off an old nest and find she has only been resting there, while if she gets off a thin one you are safe to find something, either then or soon after.

It is as well to throw down all old Woodies' (and Squirrels') nests that you go up to, for they are an awful nuisance.

Eggs.—The two eggs are milky white, oval, with both ends alike, and you can't tell them from a Horned Owl's. (I used to think I could by the texture of the shell, till I mixed mine up once too often.) The Owl *may* once in a way use a Pigeon's nest, but she would rather have something better built.

Young.—The young ones stay in the nest till they are full grown, and if you care about baby-killing (which I don't) you may make good pies of them, for they are far too common and do a lot of damage to crops. In their first plumage they have no " ring," but have wing-bars like the old ones.

Season.—They begin before the end of March in a good year, and go on with brood after brood till September or thereabouts, even later at times.

Noise.—Just one caution about Woodpigeons. If you are in a wood where you are not welcome, go very quietly and don't set the whole lot off at once, clapping their wings and telling everyone within half a mile that you are there.

2.—THE STOCK DOVE.

Bird.—Very like a Woodpigeon, but smaller, and without the white " ring " or wing-bars. You *may* see a flock of them in Winter, but then they are much commoner in the South than in the North. The breeding birds turn up about the middle of March, and scatter over the countryside, a pair here and a pair there, but never many together.

Haunts.—The favourite place for a Stock Dove's nest is a cliff such as Jackdaws or Kestrels like, but it may be just a little scarp of rock by the side of some burn, and the general rule is one crag one nest. They are often called " Rock Pigeons " in the hills, where they nest nowhere but in rocks, but lower down you may find a nest in a rabbit hole in some sand-cliff or in a *hole* in a tree, but never among the branches like a Woodpigeon's.

Nest.—They make the usual flat sort of nest, though I *once* found the eggs just laid among ivy on a very narrow rock-ledge, most likely because there was really not room for a nest there.

FIG. 19—YOUNG PEREGRINES

(see page 132)

FIG. 20—YOUNG BARN OWLS
(*see page* 136)

Eggs.—Not quite so big as a Woodie's, and *creamy* white, so you can't mistake them.

Season.—They begin about the end of April, and have several broods, or always two.

3.—THE ROCK DOVE.

Bird.—This is a blue pigeon with two dark bars on the wing and a white patch above the tail. It is from this bird that all our tame Pigeons have been bred, Homers, Tumblers, Pouters and the rest; and where Pigeons are left to take care of themselves you often see birds that have gone back to the exact colours of their wild ancestors. It is not uncommon for these birds to go wild, and nest in rocks, but you must not mistake them for truly wild Rock Doves.

Haunts.—They *only* breed on the coast, in caves as a rule, and are not common anywhere except in parts of Ireland and the West of Scotland.

Nest.—This pigeon does not always use twigs for its nest, as there are often no trees where it breeds, but grass and seaweed do as well. The birds sit fairly well, and you should be near enough to see just where the nests are before they fly off.

Eggs.—The eggs are pure white, rather smaller than a Woodpigeon's and generally rounder.

Season.—From the end of March to September.

4.—THE TURTLE DOVE.

Bird.—This is a smaller bird, with a long wedge-shaped tail which has the tips of the feathers white; and it flies much more slowly than the others. Its "coo" is a gentle purring sound which will make you think of Turtle Doves even if you have never seen one.

Haunts and Nesting-place.—It is common enough in the South, but seldom reaches Yorkshire. I believe it sometimes nests in hedges, but its regular haunts are thick copses with plenty of underwood. It chooses the same sort of nesting-place as a Jay, well hidden among the leaves, but I have never seen a nest at any great height, and it is often in a place that would not support a Jay's nest. I have seen one in a festoon of brambles that could not be reached without upsetting the eggs, though not ten feet up.

Nest.—The nest is made of fine twigs, and is so flimsy that you can nearly always see the eggs through it. These are so small that they cannot be mistaken for any other Pigeon's, and *creamy* white.

Season.—Turtle Doves arrive in May and begin laying in June, but still often manage to rear a second brood.

This is the last of the Tree Birds.

I have put the Ground birds in three families, first the Game Birds, which have some points in common with Pigeons, next the Rails, some of which are rather like the Game Birds, and lastly the Waders. Most of these Ground Birds are good to eat, and except for the Pigeons and the Ducks, all the birds that are shot for sport belong to this group.

FAMILY XXIII.
THE GAME BIRDS.

These birds are pretty near relations to our Barn-door fowls, and though they don't all *scratch* for their food, that is what their feet are meant for. Their habit is to crouch when danger threatens, and some of them are coloured so that they can make themselves invisible almost anywhere. They have short rounded wings as a rule and make a loud whirring noise when they fly—and many of them only fly when they must.

Many of the birds in this family do not pair, but one cock goes with several hens, just as it is in the farm-yard; and when this is so the cock birds are very different from the hens, and often have spurs like a game cock's, as they have to fight for their wives, and very good fighters they are. I have known a cock Pheasant to get into a pen of game-hens and kill every cock that was brought against him, till at last the owner got tired of it and put in a cock with a pair of steel spurs on, who soon made an end of the unfortunate Pheasant, but it was hardly a fair trick to play on him.

All the game-birds nest on the ground, and make very little *nest* at all. They lay a lot of eggs, which take about three weeks to hatch, and the chicks are able to run about as soon as they come out, and are well covered with down, like chickens. They grow quill feathers very soon, and can fly before they are a quarter grown, and have several new sets of quills while they are growing.

One point you will notice about Game eggs is, that when there are any markings on them at all, they are all on the surface, with none of those under-markings that you see in so many birds' eggs.

I.—THE GROUSE.

Bird.—In books he is the Red Grouse, but at home he is more likely to be called the Moorcock, and his family Moorfowl or " Moorpoots " (poults). His great distinction is that he is the only all-British bird, not found anywhere outside of the British Isles.

Cock and hen are very much the same, for these birds not only pair, but seem not to pair again if they lose their first mate, to judge by the number of single old birds one sees about a moor.

I hardly need tell you where their haunts are, for when you hear the old cocks saying in plain English " Go back, go back, go back " you will know you are getting near them.

Signs.—Finding their nests is not so easy, and you will only come on them by chance as you walk across the heather. If you constantly see pairs of birds rising together, it is no good looking for nests where they get up, for they have not begun to sit yet, though there may be eggs about if you knew where to look, and you can tell when they are laying by the extra big droppings that the hen birds make, which you are sure to see among the heather. I suppose this must happen with all birds that are laying, but it is among Grouse that you notice it most.

When you see single cocks getting up (you can tell them by their cackle) then you know the hens are sitting, and presently one gets up at your feet with a great flurry, and there is your first Grouse's nest.

Nest.—Most of them are well-hidden among long heather though often close to the edge of a short patch; and though I have seen a few that were well lined with long grass, where it grew near, the usual nest is just a scrape in the ground with practically no lining at all.

Eggs.—The eggs average seven to eight, and more than nine is a very uncommon clutch. They are creamy-white, thickly mottled with dark chocolate-brown, or sometimes red, and the colour comes off so easily that you can generally tell about how long the bird has been sitting by the amount she has scraped or brushed off them.

Young.—The chicks are golden yellow and very pretty little things. You will be surprised to see a whole brood get up and fly when they are little bigger than sparrows. The old birds are very faithful and take good care of them, and the broods keep together till about September (if Man doesn't interfere). Then the young ones collect into packs, and the old birds sit about in twos and threes, glad to be rid of them.

Season.—Towards the end of April is the usual time, but it may be sooner or later according to the weather.

2.—BLACKGAME.

Birds.—In books they call them " Black Grouse," but on their own fells they are " greyfowl " in their young days and " Blackgame " after they are grown up and fit to shoot.

These birds do not pair, and the cock is so different from the hen that a stranger to them would never believe they were the same species. He is the biggest gamebird in these parts, and often weighs four or five pounds, while I have never seen a grouse as much as two pounds. He is all black except for some white on the wing, inside the wing, and under the tail, and this curls outwards in a way that you can't mistake if one flies over you.

The Blackcock's wives are not quite so big as he is, and are called Greyhens, though they are really more brown than grey and are often shot in mistake for Grouse.

Habits.—In Spring you will often hear a curious bubbling noise, especially in the early morning, which reminds you rather of a Turkey-cock's music, and if you go to see what it is all about you will find an old Blackcock on some bare grassy knoll or open space, showing off before his wives (who are generally bored with the whole thing). What he does you can see for yourselves, and I don't think *you* will be bored. At other times you may come on two old cocks fighting, and when the hens are sitting you may see a group of cocks practising their steps, and this is a sight worth seeing, too.

Haunts and Nest.—They haunt the moors, but the white ground rather than the heather, and their nests are hidden among bracken or rushes or bent, very often on a steep bank, and too often nearer the burn than is safe, when a flood comes. They are fond of open woods too, if there are any near the moor, and you may find a nest there, perhaps under the shelter of a fallen tree, or in any low cover there is. It is just a scrape, hardly lined at all.

Eggs.—The eggs are from six to ten, much bigger than a Grouse's and brownish-yellow with small spots of dark and light brown.

Season.—The eggs are not often laid before the middle of May, and take about four weeks to hatch. The young ones are all like their mother at first, and it is not till about the 1st of September that the cocks begin to grow their black feathers. When they are nearly all black they leave the brood and skulk among the rushes till they are full-feathered, and by October they are beginning to collect in Packs for the Winter.

3.—THE PHEASANT.

This is not an ancient Briton, but as he was brought over before William the Conqueror he is as British as most of us. That is the old black-necked breed; the white-collared bird was brought from China a good deal later, and several other kinds have been introduced at different times.

You can see Pheasants every day, and I think you all know that they don't pair, and the difference between cock and hen. The cocks are great fighters, but it is only at mating time that you see them at it in earnest— in Summer it is only sparring. They crow a good deal, and in Spring you will hear and see them drumming with their wings as well. They have two curious habits, one is to crow whenever there is a heavy concussion, like blasting or big guns firing, and the other to crow when they get up into a tree to roost, just as if they wanted poachers to know where to find them.

Their wings are short, but they can use them pretty well, and in a thick wood will shoot up between the trees like rockets when they are disturbed. But if left to themselves they would always walk unless they had to cross a river or get up into a tree, and it is remarkable that they are very cunning in slipping away from danger *on their feet*, but once on the wing will fly straight home regardless of guns placed in full view to take toll of them as they pass overhead.

Nesting-haunts and Habits.—Though Pheasants roost and shelter in the woods, they generally come out both to feed and to nest, and you will find them nesting along the hedge-bottoms, in the fields, and among any kind of thick low cover. The nests are usually well hidden, but you will find some in very foolish places such as an open ditch by the roadside.

They seem very casual, often laying in each other's nests, or in Partridges', and forgetting which is their own; so that you may find one nest deserted, and the next with two birds squabbling for the right to sit, or even sitting side by side! But I must leave you something to find out about Pheasants' nests.

They are easily disturbed at first, but when hatching-time draws near they are good sitters, and will let you photograph them or do anything you like.

Nest Feathers.—The nest is a scrape in the ground, lined with a little dry grass as a rule, and always contains a few of the bird's feathers. This is the way with all game-birds, and when you come across a mixed lot of eggs (I have known it happen with Greyhens as well as with Pheasants and Partridges), you can tell the real owner of the nest by the feathers in it. If you find a Partridge has been laying in the Pheasant's nest, you have struck something out of the common, for it is generally the other way on; in fact if you look carefully you will most likely find a few Partridge feathers at the bottom, showing that a Partridge started the nest and was turned out by the Pheasant.

Eggs.—Naturally, the number of eggs in different nests varies, but 12 is a fair average, and 16 nothing out of the way when a bird puts all her eggs in the same nest, while if the neighbours have been helping—well, I'll leave you to count them. They are pale olive-brown, without markings. You often see pale blue eggs among them, but I have never seen a whole clutch that colour.

Season.—They begin to lay about mid-April, sit about 24 days, and the first young ones should be out early in June. The hen has to look after them herself, for the cock takes no interest in any of his families, and she loses a good many in ditches, etc., for she hasn't much sense, and if the first gets over all right will trot on and forget about the rest—and I don't think birds can count anyhow. The young ones grow slowly, and it is nearly November before they are really grown up.

4.—THE PARTRIDGE.

Bird.—You all know a Partridge by sight, and his ordinary call of "Chissick"; his pairing note is much the same but more rasping and long-drawn. Partridges pair, and you can't tell the difference between cock and hen on the wing. The cock is such a good father that I suspect he sometimes takes a turn with the eggs, though I have never seen him on the nest; you might look out for him. The easiest way to recognize which it is on the nest is to look at the top of the head, the cock's is bright chestnut, but the hen's speckled.

Nests.—The nests may be anywhere, but a hedge-bottom is a favourite place. You may also find them pretty often in small belts of wood, gorse coverts, hay-fields, rough grass, or scrubby places generally. The nest is always well hidden, and has often more lining in it than most Game-birds use; and a Partridge covers up her eggs when she leaves them of her own accord.

Habits.—The Partridge is a very good sitter, and on many Partridge manors the keepers take the eggs and let the birds sit on sham ones; the eggs are put in an incubator till they are just chipping, and then exchanged for the sham ones, but the sitting birds are given 20 to 30 chipped eggs to hatch, and make no objection, so you can see how tame they are. When they are near hatching you can take an egg from under one to see if it is chipped, and put it back, without her doing more than grunt and blink her eye at you. But you must not try this unless you *know* she has been sitting nearly three weeks, and of course it must be done very gently.

Eggs.—Partridges lay a lot of eggs, and from 16 to 20 is the usual nest-full. When a Pheasant has a lot of eggs you may see them lying one on top of the other, but a Partridge's are neatly arranged round and round the hollow, till the top row are perhaps sticking up above the rim. I have known one have 17 of her own and 7 given her by a Pheasant, and hatch every one. The eggs are the same colour as a Pheasant's, but smaller and more pointed. I don't think the shape ever varies, and they don't lay the blue kind of egg to my knowledge.

Season.—They pair very early, sometimes before the end of January, but wait for the grass to grow and seldom begin to lay before the second week of May. As they have a lot of eggs to lay they seldom start to sit before June, and hatching-time is the week following Midsummer Day. That is when sportsmen and keepers pray for fine weather, as a thunderstorm or two will nearly wipe out the lot.

The coveys keep together all the season as a rule, and only break up at pairing-time, and the same covey may be seen feeding in the same stubble field every day till the field is ploughed—so we may safely say that partridges have no instinct for migration, and neither have the first three Game-birds.

But this is not true of *all* the family, for the next bird is one that travels right across Europe and Asia, and was very useful to the Israelites in the Wilderness—I daresay some of their Quails were hatched in England.

5.—THE QUAIL.

Migration.—The big rush of these birds gets no further than the North of France, but *some* cross the Channel every spring, and there is no reason why you shouldn't find a nest, with luck.

Bird.—A Quail is about half as big as a Partridge and much the same colour, except for the cock's whiskers, which you won't see often. He sits very close, and when he does rise seems to have no tail at all and steers rather a crooked course, but flies pretty fast.

Call.—You are about as likely to see *him* as a Corncrake, but fortunately he has a peculiar whistle which seems to say " Quick-be-quick " in a loud whisper. He doesn't give this much in the daytime, but chiefly at dawn and dusk. There were lots of them on the Somme, and if they started saying that as you were crawling in from No Man's Land with the sky just turning grey, it sounded very like good advice. Of course his call won't help you much unless you know the common birds' voices well enough to notice a strange one, and I have heard it in my young days and just put it down as " some small bird " and thought no more about it; but if you are on the look-out for it, it is unmistakable.

Pairing.—Any that you come across will probably be just a single pair, but where there are a good many of them they more often go one cock to two or three hens; and there is a good deal of fighting among them when they first arrive, which is generally well on in May.

Nest.—They nest in corn-fields, hay-fields, or rough pastures, and the nest is much like others of the family, and well hidden.

Eggs.—The eggs are from eight to twelve, small and yellow with dark-brown markings, either spots or blotches. If you find a nest by accident you might take it for some kind of crake, but remember the Rails all build good nests, and their eggs have the grey under-markings, while Game-birds are wanting in both these points.

Season.—It is not much good looking for *eggs* before June, but you can be on the lookout for signs of the birds before that.

6.—THE RED-LEGGED PARTRIDGE.

This is a bird that was introduced about 150 years ago, and there are plenty of them in the Southern and Eastern counties, but they don't spread to the North, and soon disappear when they are turned down there. They are generally called " Frenchmen " but their proper home is Italy and Spain (and the very South of France) so that is probably why they don't care for the North.

Bird.—The Red-leg is not a bit like the other Partridge, his plumage is all plain colours and not speckled. His back is red-brown, head and flanks blue-grey with dark bars on the flanks, and under-parts fawn-coloured. His call reminds you of a very excited Guinea-fowl, and if you whisper " O-tăkă-too " quickly you get something like it.

Nest, Etc.—The nest is made in the same sort of places as a Partridge's, the eggs are bigger and have light-brown markings, and the time is about the beginning of May.

There are two other British Game-birds, but both nest a long way North.

7.—THE CAPERCAILLIE.

Generally called "Caper."

The biggest Game-bird we have—an old cock is as big as a good Turkey. They are very like Blackgame in most ways, but live in the woods. The nest is on the ground in a wood, and the eggs are like a Greyhen's, but bigger, and laid often by May 1st.

8.—THE PTARMIGAN.

Like a small Grouse, but has a lot of white about it and turns nearly all white in Winter. Lives on mountain tops, and has eggs very like a Grouse's, which are not often laid before June.

FAMILY XXIV.
THE RAILS.

These birds are great runners, and when running they stretch their necks out well in front and look anything but graceful. You can see their likeness to the Game-birds at once, but apart from their running they are a mixed lot, and two of them have taken to the water and are beginning to have webbed feet, but you can't mistake them for Ducks or Gulls or any of the true water birds. When danger threatens a Rail does not squat like a Partridge, but sprints for the nearest cover and hides. The family nesting habits are to build good solid nests, lay eight or ten eggs, and generally have two broods. The young ones are covered with black down, whatever colour their parents may be, and are able to run or swim the moment they come out.

The Rails are weak fliers, and never do it if there is any other way out of a difficulty.

1.—THE CORN CRAKE OR LANDRAIL.

Habits.—Everyone has heard this bird, but there are lots of people who have never see one at all. It is one of our latest Summer birds, often not arriving before the second week of May, by which time the grass is generally long enough to hide it, and it keeps well out of sight, though it sometimes wanders out into the open, especially in the early morning, when I have often seen them running about on lawns, and once even in a stable yard.

Bird.—It is sandy coloured all over, with streaky back and barred flanks, and you generally see it running about with neck and body all in one straight line, or standing bolt upright, but looking extraordinarily slim either way. If it is driven to use its wings by a dog it flaps along very low, with legs hanging down behind and so slowly that I have known a spaniel to chase one and catch it in the air. And yet they all go South of the Mediterranean for the Winter.

Nest.—The nests are more often in hay than in corn, and a good many of them are spoilt by the mower, as the eggs are seldom hatched before hay-time. The bird sits tight, but often escapes while the eggs get smashed, as the nest is not a mere hollow like a Partridge's, but is often built up like a Waterhen's, chiefly of grass, coarse outside and finer within. There are generally a few dead leaves for lining.

Eggs.—The eggs are from seven to ten, yellowish-white, polished, and marked with three colours, grey below, light and dark brown on top. The marks are generally oval spots or streaks running the long way of the egg. I don't think they ever vary much, and you can hardly mistake them.

Young.—It is a surprising thing to see the old Corn Crakes with their family of little black balls of fluff, and I hope you may see it. If you catch a young one you will see that he is not really black, but a beautiful dark bronze-brown.

Season.—I have only known one to have eggs before June, and then there were only two in the nest on May 28th; no second brood, of course.

Hints.—It is not an easy matter to get a Corn Crake's egg, as you can't go trampling about in hay-fields. If you should hear one calling constantly in a pasture field I think you are more likely to find its nest among the nettles in the hedge-bottom than in a thick tuft out in the field, but try both places. Another place where there are often Corn Crakes is a young plantation where the little trees are smothered in long grass, and if you are careful of the trees there is no reason why you shouldn't hunt there. Only go early in the morning, for the owners are sure to think you are there on purpose to spoil the trees.

If you can't find your Corn Crake honestly, the only way is to be on the spot when they are cutting the grass, make friends with the men, and walk round behind the mower, for if you can spot the nest in the standing stuff before the machine goes over it, you have a much better chance of getting the eggs unbroken.

2.—THE WATER RAIL.

Bird.—Just about the size of a Corn Crake, but looking like a small Waterhen. It is dark mottled brown above and dark iron grey below, with some narrow white bars on the flanks and a patch of buff under the tail; it has a red bill, longer than a Corn Crake's, and long green legs.

Habits.—It is just as shy of being seen as the last bird, and runs like a rat. It can swim and dive, but would rather hide on land. It never flies far, and I have seen one, flushed from a clump of rushes in a ditch, fly a hundred yards or so and settle on the bare hedge-bank. It seemed to have reached the end of its tether as far as flying went, and seeing no cover within reach, just sat down where it was. I walked right up to it and caught it.

Haunts.—They are Northern birds, and though we have plenty in Winter, they are not common in the breeding season. Still, any swamp where the cover is thick may hold a nest, and *if* you know it is there you ought to be able to find it.

Cries.—You will never *see* them unless you have a dog that will hunt them out, and he is very apt to *catch* them, when their preparations for nesting will most likely stop for good; but fortunately they are noisy birds, and if you know their cries you can soon tell when they are about. One noise they make is rather like a rabbit squealing in a trap, starting at its loudest and dying away, and the other is a sort of grunt, something like a frog's croak. This is not a good description, but it may help you to recognize them if you hear them.

Nest.—The nest is amongst thick rushes, sedge or other swamp growth, and is built of dead sedge and such-like, well made and solid. It is very hard to find as a rule, but if you poke about a bit, you *may* see the birds come out and show themselves, and if they do that, you are very near it. Water Rails are close sitters, but may easily slip off right at your feet and run away without being seen, and unless you are standing by the nest and they think you have found it, they do not show up.

Fig. 21—Brown Owl

(see page 137)

FIG. 22. WATERHEN
(see page 162)

Eggs.—The eggs are about seven, yellowish-white like a Corn Crake's, but with only two colours on them, reddish and grey, just a few small spots. You can hardly take them for a Corn Crake's, but I have known that bird to nest in a bed of rushes on a moor, so if you find a doubtful nest, sit down by it for a while and the birds are sure to come and have a look at you, and if you only see a red beak it will tell you what you want to know.

Season.—The laying season for these birds is generally May, and as eggs have been found in July I think they must try a second brood when they are not too late in beginning.

3.—THE SPOTTED CRAKE.

Bird.—This is a very rare bird indeed, but it does breed in the North occasionally. It is a smaller bird than a Corn Crake, like it in colour, but rather a darker brown, and has white spots on the breast. In habits it is like a Water Rail and much quieter, having only a very gentle call, " Kwit, kwit," which you might never notice at all; so, unless you have a dog to rout them out, you stand a poor chance of knowing when there is one about.

Nest.—The nest is generally *in* the water, but built up well above it like a Waterhen's, either in a tussock or amongst reeds or other growth; and the bird slips off quietly like the rest of them.

Eggs.—The eggs are boldly spotted with dark reddish-brown, with some lighter markings, and the inside of the shell shows green, so you ought to know them if you are lucky enough to get them. There ought to be about 10 in an average clutch.

Season.—Its time is about the same as the Corn Crake's, any time after June 1st.

4.—BAILLON'S CRAKE.

A smaller bird again, like the last, but without the spots. It has apparently stopped breeding in England, but may begin again. Its nest is like a Water Rail's, and its eggs brownish and speckled all over. It is said to start laying in May, and have two broods.

5.—THE WATERHEN (Fig. 22).

Or Moorhen.

Bird.—No need to describe this common bird, but you can always tell it when swimming by its slowness, cocked-up tail showing the white underneath, and way of jerking its head at each stroke. It has a red and yellow beak, and a red sort of shield covering its forehead.

Habits.—Its feet are slightly fringed to give them more power in the water, but on land it runs about as fast as the other Rails. It is just about as fond of hiding, too, especially in the water, where I have caught them by hand, lurking under a trailing branch or a lot of floating rubbish, with just the bill up to breathe with. They are astonishingly hard to see like that, even when you have seen them go there. Once when I surprised one in a small ditch it dived and stuck its head into the mud at the side, about a foot under water. There it seemed to be prepared to stay till it drowned, but after giving it two minutes I pulled it out, and it flew away much as usual. I sometimes wonder whether they have some way of breathing when they are stuck in the mud like that, and if I see one do it again I shall allow her 10 minutes to settle the question.

Haunts.—Every pond, most streams, and a good many ditches have Waterhen's nests, so you need never go far to find one.

Spare Nests.—If you go early you are sure to find a lot of nests just beginning, for they start a good many before they decide on one to lay in. In fact they often start to lay in an unfinished nest, and add to the lining as they add to the family. The other nests do for dry docks for the said family later on, after they are launched.

Nesting-places.—The regular place for the nest is in a clump of sedge, rushes, flags or other growth out in the water, or now and then on the bank. Often by a stream it is in the branches of a willow overhanging the water, and from that you come to thorn bushes on the bank, holly bushes, and trees up to 20 feet high, only very occasionally of course.

Nest.—The nest is well built up of sedge, flags, or whatever is on the spot, and the eggs are kept well above the water and quite dry. Often you will see dead leaves in the lining, such as a Dipper uses. If a pond's level rises the birds will build their nests up so as to keep above it.

Eggs.—The eggs are from six to ten, buff-coloured with reddish-brown spots, and you may get five or six different varieties. The shell is very thick and hard.

Young.—The young ones are out in about three weeks and go straight from the egg to the water as a rule. I found a nest once, some way back from the water's edge, with the young ones just struggling out of the eggs, so I thought I would have a photograph of them, but they kept popping over the side faster than I could put them back, and I never managed to get them all together, though there were only six. They have little red plates on their foreheads at first, like the old ones, but these turn green as they grow up. When they come out of the egg they can swim *and* dive as if they had been at it all their lives (I suppose they have really).

Problem.—If you ever find a nest in a tree, not exactly above the water, you should try to be there at hatching time and see how the young ones get away. I have never seen it myself, but I know their instinct is to go overboard at once, and in one case I saw the brood swimming about in the stream, one addled egg in the nest, and no mangled corpses at the foot of the tree. The question is, do the old ones carry them down, and if so, how?

Season.—Waterhens begin to lay about the middle of April, and don't wait for the weeds to grow, if they are late (that is when they are most likely to build in hedges or trees). I think they always have a second brood.

6.—THE COOT.

"Bell coot" or "Bell poot."

Bird.—This is a ground bird that "lives in the water and practically never comes ashore." But even if it is a water bird it is a Rail, and very like a Waterhen to look at. It has a white plate on its head where the Waterhen has a red one, and that is how it got the two names I have given above, which mean "Bald coot" and "Bald hen," otherwise it is black all over except for a narrow white bar on the wing. Its toes have lobes of skin like the Grebes' for swimming with, and so it is a stronger swimmer than the Waterhen; and it is also a stronger flier and a bigger bird.

Habits.—It is very different from the rest of them in habits, for it swims about in the open, and is quite willing to fly, though when it does it runs along the top of the water to get going, which is just what all the Rails do, on land or water, when they want to fly.

Haunts.—It likes big ponds and lakes, and slow-running rivers, with plenty of cover at the edges, as well as plenty of open water to swim about in.

Nest.—The nest is built like a Waterhen's, but bigger, and comes even higher above the water-level. Often its foundations are on the bottom, and sometimes it floats like a Grebe's, but only in very deep water.

Eggs.—The seven or eight eggs are larger and paler than a Waterhen's, and have very small dark spots thinly scattered over them.

Season.—The Coot does wait for the weeds to grow a bit, and you will not find eggs as a rule till late in May, as the nest needs a good growth to hide it. They often have second broods for all that.

FAMILY XXV.
THE WADERS.

These birds have long slim legs and feet, with either no hind toe or a very small one, just made for running about on soft mud or paddling in shallow water. They are very graceful and dainty-looking as a rule, and nicely balanced on their feet, and can run quite fast without looking ridiculous, not a bit like the last two families. Their bills are all sizes and shapes, according to the creatures they feed on, and among them you will find both the longest and nearly the shortest of all our birds.

They nearly all have long-pointed wings and can fly fast and far, and they always take wing when anything scares them.

In this family the rule seems to be to make a very slight nest or none at all, but to hide it or not as you like; then you must lay four very big pear-shaped eggs, and arrange them with the points inwards, and when the young ones come out they are well covered with down, and they can run about and almost look after themselves. They do one thing very well, which their parents certainly don't teach them, for it is not in *their* line at all, and that is they crouch and hide so cleverly that it generally takes a dog's nose to find them. They seem to have learnt that trick while they were in the big egg, where they certainly grow more than other birds do in theirs though they only take three weeks to hatch. Before they are out of the egg they make their voices heard, and I have stopped short in a wood by the river to listen to some Sandpipers calling in the distance, only to find that the sounds came from some eggs in a nest close to my feet.

That reminds me that I ought to have told you that most of these birds have clear piping cries, and when you know a few of them you can generally tell whether a new call is a Wader's or not.

I.—THE STONE CURLEW.

"Norfolk Plover" or "Thick-knee."

These are not North-country names, as the bird comes no further North than the Yorkshire Wolds, and is rare there; Norfolk is the best place to find it.

Bird.—It is sandy-coloured, showing two white bars on the wing when flying, which it does rather like a

Pigeon. Its thick joints you will not notice unless you catch a young one. It gives a whistling cry something like a Curlew's, but looks nothing like one, having quite a short beak.

It does not keep the family rules very well, for it sometimes squats instead of flying away, and only lays two eggs, which are not pear-shaped, but rounded.

Haunts and Nest.—It haunts open commons and heaths, where it nests on the bare ground, sandy or gravelly for choice. There is no nest, only a hollow in the ground, and the bird slips off as it sees you coming generally running some distance before it flies, though it may rise from the eggs if you come on it suddenly from close at hand.

Eggs.—The two eggs are buff-coloured with brown blotches and streaks, and as big as a Golden Plover's. Their number, rounded shape, and the nest will tell you what they are.

Season.—This is a Summer bird, and does not have eggs much before June.

2.—THE PEEWIT.

Lapwing or Green Plover.

Bird.—Everyone must know this common bird, with its wheeling flight and rounded wings, so very different from most of the Waders. One of the signs of Spring is when you hear its cry of " Pee-wit " or (" Tew-fit " as they call it in Yorkshire) change to the pairing note, " Pees-weep-weep-weep." Out on the moors where Peewits are Summer birds only the people call them " Pees-weeps," for that is the call they hear most.

This is the only Wader that carries a crest, and if you get close enough to see the beautiful shading of green on his back you will see that he is a much handsomer bird than he looks in the distance.

Nest.—Peewits nest everywhere except on the very highest fells, so you may find them in any kind of bare field, plough, stubble, or grass, and on the open moor on burnt ground, or very short heather, but it must be bare ground without any cover. The nest is a shallow round scrape made by the birds themselves, and you can often watch them doing it, turning round and round with breast down and tail in the air. Round the edge are a few bits of straw as a rule, and now and then you see one regularly built up at the sides. The first egg is often laid at this stage and lies on the bare earth, but by the time all four have arrived you will find them on a bed of straw or grass, thick enough to keep them off the cold ground.

" Sham " Nests.—If you should find several nests scratched out but not lined, don't be too sure that the birds have not begun to lay yet; if you persevere along the same line, or the same level on a slope, you may easily find a nest with eggs, as they often make quite a number of beginnings before they fix on one for laying.

Habits.—The bird leaves her nest the moment she sees you in the distance, and runs a long way before she rises, but if you suddenly appear within 100 yards or less, she flies off in a hurry, keeping low and going straight (thus you can tell her from a cock bird, whom you will most likely see standing up before he rises, and who generally mounts up in the air at once). So the best place to find Plovers' nests is broken ground, or small fields divided by walls, where you are always coming suddenly on new ground.

If you have to hunt over big fields you have more trouble in finding them, for they may be 20 yards from the fence or right out in the middle. The best places to look are along the side of any ridge there may be, and pretty close to a ditch or stream if there is one.

Near the moors they are fond of those grass fields with low, flat tussocks all over them, and here the nest is always on a tussock and never in a hollow; and in the same way they often make a nest on an old mole-hill.

Eggs.—The four very pear-shaped eggs are olive-brown with dark brown or black markings, generally blotches, sometimes spots, and very rarely streaks. I have only found three nests with five eggs among a few thousand, and in one of *them* the fifth was so different that it had evidently been laid by another bird.

Protective Colouring.—The wonderful thing about these eggs is that they match whatever sort of ground they are laid on, and are always hard to see (a Partridge's plumage is the same, invisible on grass and plough alike). An empty nest is far easier to see than one with eggs in, and the better it is built the better you you can spot it, eggs or no eggs.

Season.—They begin laying at the very end of March in an early year, and have no second brood as a rule though you will often find nests as late as June on the high ground. These, I think, belong to birds that have been robbed several times.

3.—THE GOLDEN PLOVER (Fig. 23).

Bird.—He is very different from the Green Plover, and has the pointed wings and swift straight flight that a Wader ought to have. His head, back and wings are spotted with golden yellow, but like a starling he looks quite dull in the distance, and the things you will know him by are, first, his breast, which is nearly all black in Summer, and second, his way of sitting up on a tussock and piping at you, just a single " pee-e " which has a very mournful sound. He has another call which you may hear up in the air, and which seems to say " Come he-e-ere," but when you hear that it means they are just pairing and it is too soon for eggs.

Haunts.—He is a Northern bird, not found much south of Yorkshire in Summer, and his haunts are the higher moors. I have never seen a nest that wasn't among bent or heather.

Nest.—The nest is never hidden on purpose, but may be built among longer stuff than a Peewit likes, and so is often half hidden by grass or heather.

Habits.—These birds leave their nests in much the same fashion as a Peewit does, and are more likely to take warning from the cries of the other moorland birds as you approach, so that you often find them coming to meet you and sitting on tufts, looking very anxious though the nest is nowhere near. If you *are* near the nest they do much the same, and try to draw you away from it, and when they have young ones, often play the broken wing trick, so it is as well to have a good look round near you when they seem very anxious.

You can watch the birds a long time without finding their nests, and even if they go to it they are almost invisible on the ground; so your best way is to take advantage of broken ground and try to surprise them. If you can go *on a wet day* to a place where there are a good many breeding, you are safe to find a nest or two.

Eggs.—The four eggs are bigger and glossier than a Peewit's, not so pear-shaped, and the ground-colour yellower, otherwise they are very much alike.

Season.—You will not often find eggs before the middle of May, but I *have* known them to lay nearly a month earlier.

4.—THE DUNLIN.

Bird.—The Dunlin is about half the size of a Golden Plover, with a brown back and a black patch on the middle part of its breast. Its flight is more fluttering, and it has a similar sort of pipe, but not so loud or so long, and it has also a sort of purring note which you will hear if you get amongst them.

Haunts.—It is a rare bird in Summer, though common on the sea-shore in Winter. You will find a few breeding here and there on the mosses of the higher fells of Northumberland, and on suitable marshes near the sea, such as you find in the Solway; and where you see them one year there is pretty sure to be a nest the next.

Nest.—The nest is generally on marshy ground, but well out of the wet on a tuft of grass, rushes or heather. It is open as a rule, but sometimes well hidden, and has only a slight lining of grass.

Habits.—The bird sits fairly close, though she often slips off the nest and runs a little way before flying. When you are at the nest both birds will come and sit about near you, purring and preening themselves, but they may do this far away from their nest as well, and if you see a pair it is very little good watching them in the hope that they will show you where the nest is, but you should search every tuft near you in case you have got near the nest unawares. If only one bird appears, keep on walking about with your eyes open, for the other is probably still on the nest.

Eggs.—The eggs are four, or often only three, olive with bold brown markings, and rather like a Snipe's but much smaller, no bigger than a Magpie's.

Season.—They begin to lay at the very beginning of May, but eggs may be found much later.

5.—THE DOTTEREL.

Haunts.—This is a very rare bird indeed, but you just *might* find a nest on the top of one of the Lake Mountains (or even the Cheviots, though I have never heard of them nesting there).

Bird.—The bird is bigger than a Dunlin, but still small for a Plover, and you will know it by a white band like a Ring-ousel's but lower down, a chestnut patch on the breast below that, and a black one lower still, on the belly. Its back is sandy brown, and it has a white stripe over the eye. Its note is a low whistle without any expression in it.

It is one of the tamest birds there are, and that is how it has got so rare; if you do come across any you will have no difficulty in getting a good look at them.

Nest.—The nest is just a hollow in the grass or moss often beside a stone. The bird is said to sit closely when she has been at it for some time, but earlier she slips off like other birds that have open nests.

Eggs.—The eggs are almost always three, with dark markings on a yellowish ground. They are about the size of a Snipe's, but not so pear-shaped as a rule, and sometimes nearly round.

Season.—They are laid late, in June or even July.

6.—THE RINGED PLOVER.
Or Ringed Dotterel.

Haunts.—This little bird nests on the sea-shore, and is fairly common there, and a few come up the rivers to breed in some places.

Bird.—It is easily recognized by a white ring round the neck, with a black band below.

Nest and Eggs.—They often nest in small colonies, but the nests are at least 10 yards apart, not close together like the Terns', they are nothing more than hollows scraped in the sand above high-water mark, and the four small eggs are sand-coloured with small black spots, and very hard to see, as they match the sand perfectly.

Habits.—You will hardly ever see the birds get off their nests, so when you see them about you should pick the likeliest stretch of sand and walk about with your eyes on the ground, very slowly and carefully, as it is quite easy to tread on a nest even when you are looking for them.

Season.—The season for these birds is very uncertain, and I have heard of a nest in early April, but the second half of May is probably the best time, and there are always some in June.

7.—THE OYSTERCATCHER.
" Sea-Pie " or " Sea Pyot."

Bird.—This is a big black and white bird with a red bill and legs, and gives a loud shrill pipe, which you cannot mistake any more than you can mistake the bird itself. The bill is stronger than most Waders' and is used for opening mussels—oysters live a bit too far under water for him to tackle.

Haunts.—Their haunts are beds of shingle, either on the shore or far up the rivers, and you may expect to find Oystercatchers wherever you find big stretches of it.

Nest.—The nest is just a scrape among the stones, and you generally find a few " sham " ones near it, as with Peewits. This bird *has* been known to nest on a ploughed field, and I have seen a photograph of a nest among the gravel on a railway track.

Eggs.—The eggs are sandy-coloured with small black spots, or often streaks. They only lay three, bigger than a Golden Plover's, and not at all pear-shaped.

You will have to search for these eggs, unless you can get quite close to the spot before the bird sees you, and you will find them very hard to see among the stones.

Season.—They often begin to lay early in May, up the rivers, but I think they are later on the coast, at any rate there are often eggs in June.

8.—THE SANDPIPER.

" Summer Snipe."

Bird.—You cannot mistake this little pale brown and white bird, which you will see skimming along the stream with his tail spread out, piping incessantly. When he settles on a stone he stretches his wings above his head, as many of the Waders do, otherwise you might almost mistake him for some kind of lark.

Haunts.—Sandpipers are as common as Dippers in the North, but stick to the larger streams and big rivers as a rule, and are seldom found right up the small burns.

Nest.—The nest is generally close to the waterside, among the grass or other cover, often in a bank, and nearly always pretty well hidden, but I have found them quite open, and even on a bare gravel-bed. It is a scrape, fairly thickly lined with dry grass as a rule.

Habits.—The bird is a good sitter unless her nest is very open, and all you have to do to find it is walk quietly along the river bank and keep your eyes open.

Eggs.—The four eggs are a sort of deep cream colour with markings of brown and often grey as well.

Season.—The birds should nearly all have eggs by June 1st. May 12th is my earliest record for four eggs, but that was a very early nest.

8.—THE REDSHANK (Fig. 24).

Bird.—This is like a big Sandpiper, but has dark wings with white patches on them, and a white rump, and sometimes looks almost black and white when flying. It flies in a zig-zag fashion, with its narrow wings very much bent, and is always piping a loud double note which you soon get to know. Its legs are more orange than red.

Haunts.—It is one of the commonest shore-birds in Winter, but in Summer goes inland, and nests in marshes, either on low ground or high, often several pairs in the same marsh.

Nest, Habits and Hints.—The nest is well hidden in a tuft, like a Snipe's, and some say the bird twists the ends of grass together over the top of it; but unlike a Snipe she rarely sits until you get near, and very often as you approach the marsh you will see both birds flying towards you, piping hard. They will keep on mobbing you as long as you are on their ground, and you can't tell by their behaviour when you are near the nest.

If there is a steep hillside overlooking the marsh, with a bit of cover on it, your best plan is to go up there and watch, and before long you should see one settle and start running among the tufts; you probably lose sight of her, but you get a good idea of whereabouts her nest is. Then if you come back *at dusk* and walk straight to that spot, you should get within five yards of the nest before the bird flies off. If you can't see a bird going home, still if you come at dusk and walk the *dry* parts round the edge and any there may be in the middle, you have a much better chance than in the daytime. It is worth while looking in tufts of rushes, for I have several times found nests in them, but the favourite place is one of those little tufts of wiry grass that grow in the drier parts of a marsh.

A good dog is a great help in finding all sorts of nests on the ground. I had a spaniel once which found me more Red-shanks' nests in nine or ten seasons than I have found for myself in half a lifetime.

Eggs.—The four eggs are the same size as a Peewit's, and marked in much the same way, but the ground colour is buff, not olive, and the markings browner. If you are in doubt, remember that 99 out of 100 Redshanks' nests are covered, and 100 out of 100 Peewits' are open. If you want to identify an egg you have found lying about, or a Corbie's leavings, hold it up to the light, you can see the spots showing through a Peewit's egg, but not through a Red-shank's

Season.—The middle of April is early enough to look for eggs, and you have small hope of finding a Redshank's nest till she has begun to sit.

FIG. 23—GOLDEN PLOVER

(see page 169)

FIG. 24—REDSHANK
(see page 175)

9.—THE CURLEW.

" Whaup " in Scotland and the Borders.

Bird.—His very long curved bill and his unmistakable whistle are enough to know him by, but as you might mistake one for a Seagull rising a long way off, I had better mention that he has a white rump which you can see nearly as far as you can see *him*.

Haunts.—Like the Redshank, he is a common shore bird in Winter, but comes inland to nest—of course he moves North as well, and the birds that breed with us mostly winter in Spain, and arrive on the moors before our shore Curlews have started for *their* breeding-grounds, which are much further North. You will never find Curlews nesting in the low country, but always on high ground, if not actually on the moor.

Nest.—The nest is like a Peewit's, only, of course, much bigger (and easier to see). On the moor it is generally on burnt ground, and if you find one in long heather you will see that the bird has made no attempt to hide it; on white ground the favourite place is on top of a tussock of bent.

Habits and Hints.—The bird's habits are just like a Peewit's, and your only chance of seeing one get off her nest is to come on her unawares. A good plan is to follow the bed of a burn if there is one, and look up on top now and then where you think there is a chance. If there is no stream, take a line which *crosses* any ridges there may be, and keep your eyes open as you top each one. You will find most nests near the top of the ridge, where the bird has a good view, and a bird rising from a hollow generally turns out to have been feeding there, in some damp patch. Of course where a stone wall crosses a likely bit of moor you can often look over in several places without alarming birds further along, unless the ground is quite level.

Eggs.—The four eggs are very big, olive green with markings of darker green and brown, and the really dark browns are rare.

Young.—They take a full month to hatch, and the young ones have straight short bills, so that you would hardly think they were Curlews, but for their voices.

Season.—You generally begin to find their eggs about the last week of April.

10.—THE WOODCOCK (Fig. 25).

Bird.—This is a beautifully mottled brown bird, which you might easily mistake for an owl on the wing, except that it always rises from the ground, starts with its legs hanging down, and makes a kind of " flip-flop " with its wings as it gets up. If you get a side view, you will see a curious square-shaped head, and a very long bill pointing downwards. It has a queer hesitating sort of flight, which you should watch carefully, as it is very useful to be able to recognize one in the dusk.

Haunts and Nest.—It nests in woods, among bracken or other cover, and sits very close; its brown plumage matching its surroundings so well that you can hardly see it, though its big round black eye often gives it away. If you want to find a nest then you must hunt very closely in the wood, especially where there are patches of bracken, though open nests are sometimes found at the foot of a tree. The nest is just a hollow, with some dead leaves in it as a rule.

A small wood of fairly young trees is a likely place, but it should not be too thick, and the nearer it is to a marsh the likelier it is to hold a Woodcock.

Habits.—You will hunt your wood more thoroughly if you *know* there is a nest there, and this you can find out by waiting outside it at nightfall. If it *is* the right wood you will see the cock bird flying round it just above the tree tops, and perhaps hear him give a sort of chuckle. After a minute or two of this his mate comes out and joins him, and they go off to feed. You may see the cock turning somersaults like a Tumbler Pigeon sometimes, high up in the air, but I don't know what his idea is unless it is pure joy.

Eggs.—The three or four eggs are not very pear-shaped, and yellowish in ground-colour, with red-brown and grey markings, either spots or blotches. You cannot mistake them for any other bird's.

Young.—The young ones are out in about three weeks, and it is said that the old birds carry them to the marsh where they feed at nights, and bring them back to the wood in the mornings. Their long bills are very good for catching worms, but hardly for carrying more than one at a time, so I expect this is quite true. I know they carry their young ones away from danger, gripping them between their knees and sometimes holding them there by pressing their bills against them.

Season.—They begin early, often in March, but the first half of April is the best time to look for them as a rule. Second broods are very uncommon, but I have known one to have fresh eggs on June 22nd.

II.—THE SNIPE.
Or "Heather-bleater."

Bird.—He has a long bill, second only to the Curlew's, and so well made for catching worms *in* the ground that he can't pick one up *on* the ground, any more than you can pick up a pin with a pair of scissors that has lost one point, for the top half is longer than the lower, so that when he feels a worm he can push straight down and catch it without wasting any time or losing touch for an instant. His back is beautifully streaked with brown and black, and his breast mostly white, but he flies so fast and crooked that he looks like a streak himself, and you will easily know him by that and his cry of " Scape ! Scape ! " which he nearly always gives when he rises (but a bird getting off her nest very rarely does it, and if one rises silently you are pretty safe to find a nest).

His breeding note is a sort of " chip-chop, chip-chop," repeated very quickly and continuously, and this he gives when sitting on the ground or on a wall or post, as well as when flying low.

Drumming.—He makes another noise called " drumming " or " bleating," which you are sure to hear in the Spring, and which you would never think was made by a bird, though you might take it for the buzz of a bee caught in the grass, or the bleating of a goat, or even the hum of a big car in the distance. It is hard to tell where the sound comes from, but when you do you will see the Snipe high up in the air, careering round in big circles. Every now and then he dives head-first with wings quivering and tail spread like a fan, and it is then that the noise is made, apparently by the outer tail-feathers vibrating in the wind of his flight, otherwise why should he spread them out? No doubt the wings help, for you can hear much the same sort of note when a Peewit is wheeling about, and when Ducks suddenly dive down from a big height, turning the quills so that the air passes through the wing.

This trick of tearing round in circles will remind you of what a Woodcock does in the evening, and show you where to look for a nest in the same way.

Haunts and Nest.—The Snipe's haunts are marshes, whether on high ground or low, but in most parts of the country he nests more among the hills than in the valleys. The nest may be on wet ground, but if so it is in some solid tuft of grass and well out of the water; more often it is on the drier land at the edge of the swamp. It is generally well hidden in a tuft of wiry grass, and the usual nest is a hollow with a very little lining of grass, but you may find one well built up occasionally, and I have a photograph of one without any lining at all.

Habits.—The bird sits tight, generally not flying off till you are near enough to see exactly where she rises, and if you only hear her, you will often see the grass above the nest still shaking if you are quick in looking round. So there is not much difficulty in finding a few nests where there are plenty of them.

Eggs.—The four eggs may be anything from dark olive brown to pale green in ground colour, so you need at least half-a-dozen varieties, but the markings are nearly always long-shaped blotches of dark brown, laid on with a spiral twist round the egg. They are proper Wader eggs, pear-shaped, and big for the bird.

Season.—Some Snipe start to lay much sooner than others, and you may find eggs by mid-April, but many more a month later.

Those are all the Waders that you have much hope of finding. I will just mention very briefly the others that nest in Britain.

12.—THE KENTISH PLOVER.

A very rare little bird which only nests in a few places on the sea-shore in Kent and Sussex. Like a Ringed Plover, but smaller still. Nest, just a scrape in the sand; eggs, three or four, dark and streaky and very hard to see; season, end of May.

13.—THE RUFF.

Used to be common in the Fens, but is now almost or quite extinct in England. The hen, or Reeve, has no ruff; her eggs and nest are very like a Redshank's, but she sits better. Season end of May or June.

14.—THE GREENSHANK.

Only breeds in the North of Scotland. Is bigger than a Redshank, but has the same sort of habits and nest. Eggs almost white, with bold brown blotches, and like no others. Lays in May.

15.—THE WHIMBREL.

Only breeds in the Outer Hebrides, Orkneys, and Shetlands. Often called "Half-Curlew," and looks it. Nest not so open, eggs like Curlew's but smaller, and season not much before June.

16.—THE RED-NECKED PHALAROPE.

Breeds in the same places as the Whimbrel. Has webs on its toes like a Coot and swims a great deal. Nests in grass or rushes near a pool, and is very tame at the nest. Eggs dark, and smaller than any other Wader's. Season June. The cock bird hatches the eggs and looks after the brood.

A lot of other Waders nest further North, and are found on our shores in Autumn or Winter. I believe there are still one or two whose nests have never been found by any British naturalist.

WATER BIRDS.

These are the birds that are evidently meant to get their living in the water, and many of them never come ashore at all except to nest. All except the Storks have webbed feet of some sort. I have taken them in this order:—

The Stork Tribe.—Long legs and big wings.
The Pelican Tribe.—Long necks and big throats.
The Duck Tribe.—Short narrow wings and flat bills.
The Gull Tribe.—Long wings and hooked bills.
The Penguin Tribe.—Feet well to the rear and long bodies.

FAMILY XXVI.
THE HERONS.

You can see a Heron wading any day, but he looks about as much like a " Wader " as you do; and if you still want to know why he is not classed with the Waders, look at his footprints by the water's edge, and you will see that his hind toe is as big as any of the others. Only one Heron nests in England.

THE HERON.

"Heronsew" or "Crane" in some parts.

Bird.—I need not tell you what he looks like, but you can tell he is a kind of Stork by the way he flies with his neck folded back and his long legs sticking out behind—most birds stretch their necks when they fly, and manage to tuck their legs out of sight (though the last is more than a Heron can be expected to manage). His cry is a harsh squawk which it is useful to know, especially when you are trying to find a heronry in a big wood.

Habits.—You will see Herons all about the rivers and streams, each fishing solemnly by itself; but for nesting they collect together, sometimes forming a big colony like Rooks, sometimes just three or four nests together, and it is only rarely that you will find a single nest—though they do seem to be deserting the old heronries rather, and scattering about more than they used to.

Haunts.—They nest in woods of tall trees, sometimes near the river and quite often well away from it, for a mile or two is nothing to their big wings, and they have been known to travel eight miles to get food for their young ones. In some heronries the trees are very stiff to climb, and if you can find a few nests in some clump of trees up a hill burn, you will probably find it easier to get up to one.

Big larches and spruce firs are the favourite trees, but any kind of tree will do so long as it is high.

Nest.—The nests are close together, sometimes two or more in the same tree; and the favourite place is on a flat branch near the top, or right at the top of a spruce, when the nest is built round the main stem to give it a grip. It is a big flat nest of sticks, often very thick and solid when it has been rebuilt a few times; and when it is at the top of a fir tree you may get underneath and not be able to reach the eggs at all, it sticks out so far all round. So you should choose one not right at the top, if you can.

Eggs.—They lay three or four eggs, pale blue and as big as a Duck's, with a rough shell.

Young.—The young ones are hatched in just under four weeks, and are able to stand up and covered with long grey down, which, along with their beaks, gives them a very quaint look. Of course both beak and legs are quite short at first.

Season.—Herons are very early birds, may have eggs by March 1st, and are almost certain to have laid by the third week. There are no second broods as far as I know, though once when I passed a heronry on May 26th I saw a fresh nest with the bird on—about two months after the others there had hatched. I expect she had had her nest spoilt somewhere else, and was making up for lost time.

Note.—You may be able to see how a Heron disposes of her legs when she wants to get down onto her eggs. I was once told by a Dignitary of the Church that they had two holes in the nest and stuck their legs through them. But I am afraid you won't see *that*, though he said *he* had (he is very short-sighted).

THE BITTERN.

Used to nest regularly in England, but is now very rare, though increasing again. I have seen Bitterns in Winter, but they generally get shot or leave the place before nesting-time. It has the Heron's bill and carriage, but its legs are much shorter and it has hooked claws. It is about the colour of a Woodcock, and will squat in the grass till you are nearly on top of it, and I got the shock of my life when one rose out of the grass at my feet where I was looking for a Jack Snipe, for the bird is a good yard from wing-tip to wing-tip. In the breeding season it makes a booming noise, which can hardly be missed, and its nest is a heap of dead reeds, etc., in the thickest cover the marsh provides. The four eggs are plain olive brown, and as big as an Oystercatcher's, and their season is any time from the end of March to the middle of May.

FAMILY XXVII.
THE CORMORANTS.

This family contains the two Cormorants and the Gannet, which all belong to the Pelican tribe, and are great fishers, though very different in their looks and ways. The cormorants are big black-looking birds, which sit about on rocks just clear of the water, and when they go fishing slip into the water without a splash and swim after their prey. The Gannet is nearly all white, haunts high cliffs like the Bass, and fishes in a way of his own, cruising about high in the air till he sees a fish near the surface, when he drops on it like a stone. The fishermen kill them by towing a board with a herring nailed on it behind their boat. The Gannet dives at the fish and breaks his neck on the board.

All these three build big nests which they keep in an extraordinarily filthy and smelly state, and their young ones are about as hideous as anything you can imagine, with bare black leathery skins. Their eggs are coated with a soft chalky layer which you can scrape off, and are a delicate green underneath.

1.—THE CORMORANT (Fig. 26).

Bird and Haunts.—This is quite a common bird round the coast, and nests on the Farnes and similar places. You can recognize him by his long wings and neck, and he often sits on a rock with one wing or both spread out to dry after he has been fishing. He is really dark green but looks black, and has a white patch on the cheeks and throat by which you may know him from the next bird.

Nests.—The nests are quite close together on the rocks, or sometimes in trees, and are made chiefly of seaweed. They are very big, and sometimes built up like pillars several feet high, so they are easy enough to find. The hollow for the eggs is generally lined with green grass or plants of some kind, but this is not enough to keep it sweet, and the whole place is covered with droppings and rotten fish, and stinks horribly.

Eggs.—I have told you about the eggs already. There are generally three, sometimes more, long and oval in shape, and they take about a month to hatch.

Season.—The laying season is from the end of April onwards, but you should always find some eggs in June.

2.—THE SHAG.
Or Green Cormorant.

Bird.—Rather smaller, bronze green in colour, and wears a forward-curling crest in Spring.

Habits, Etc.—It is not so common as the Cormorant, and has much the same habits, but nearly always builds in a cave, or at least a crevice in the rocks, making its nest big or small according to space.

Eggs.—The eggs are generally three, and only a little smaller than the last bird's.

Season.—Laying begins later, about the end of May.

3.—THE GANNET.

Or Solan Goose.

Bird.—This is a big white bird with black-tipped wings and a straight beak that looks like a Heron's.

Haunts.—We have plenty of them, but for nesting they congregate at about half-a-dozen places round the coast, such as the Bass Rock, Ailsa Craig, Lundy Island, Grassholm (Pembrokeshire), and two or three other places in the Outer Hebrides and the North Coast of Scotland. In some of these places there are hundreds of nests, all over the rock wherever they can find a ledge.

Nest.—The nest is made of seaweed and other rubbish, and as filthy as the others. You need not only a strong head but a strong stomach as well to go climbing after them.

Egg.—Only one egg is laid, like a Cormorant's, but much bigger. It takes five weeks to hatch, and the young one has a black skin, which is soon hidden by white down.

Season.—May is the time when they begin, but you will find plenty of eggs in June. That is the time to visit sea-birds' nesting-places in general.

FAMILY XXVIII.
THE DUCKS, GEESE and SWANS.

First I will dispose of the Swans. All the wild Swans breed in the Arctic, and the Mute Swans that you find about our lakes and rivers are really half-tame—though you will find they get wild enough with *you* if you try to interfere with their nests, and they are very dangerous customers, too.

Next come the Geese, which also go a long way north, but a few stay to breed in the North of Scotland and the Outer Hebrides. The only kind of Goose that does is the **Grey-lag Goose,** from which our tame Geese are descended. It builds a great big nest of sticks and other rubbish, on the ground, and lays six or more eggs, which are well packed in with down. The season is late April or early May.

Next comes a bird which is neither Goose nor Duck, but something in between:—

THE SHELDRAKE.

Bird.—A fairly common bird on the coast, where it is sandy. It is a big handsome Duck, looking piebald in the distance and close to, the most noticeable points about it are its red bill, shaped like a Goose's, and a broad chestnut band across its chest. Duck and Drake are the same colour, and take turns at sitting.

Nest.—They nest in burrows, either home-made or rabbit-made, and a good many may be found nesting close together. The hole goes a long way in, and at the end is a nest of dry grass lined with down. It is hard to find the right hole, as the birds are very shy of going to it when anyone is in sight, and the best times to see them are morning and evening, when one goes in to take a turn with the eggs, and the other comes out.

If you get the chance of watching them out in the open before the eggs are all laid, you may see something very interesting.

Eggs and Season.—The eggs are often 12 or more, creamy white, and very smooth, and laying usually begins in May.

Note.—You often see tame Sheldrakes on ponds in public parks.

THE TRUE DUCKS.

You will know Ducks on the wing by their look of having the wings set very far back, and being all head and neck and no tail, just the opposite of a Pheasant. Also their wings are short and pointed and move very fast, with a sort of whistling sound.

On the water you can tell them from other waterfowl by their way of setting their heads back, so that the breast is the most forward part of the bird; they only stretch their necks when they are suspicious, and think of flying.

All Ducks have a patch on the wing, called the speculum, generally metallic green or blue, with white edges.

They are night-feeders and fly regularly at dusk and dawn to and from their feeding haunts, and in the daytime you will often see them sleeping, either ashore or afloat.

The Drake is always a much more handsome bird than the Duck, who does all the sitting and generally looks after the young brood herself. The Drake begins to moult his fine feathers quite early in the Summer, and puts on what is called his " eclipse " plumage, very like his wife's. About July he casts all his quills at once and cannot fly for a fortnight or so, and that is the height of his eclipse, when he skulks among the rushes as if he was really ashamed of himself; but after that he begins to smarten up, and by October is his old self again with his full Winter plumage.

All the Ducks are dingy brown, all their nests are much the same, and their eggs only vary from pale green to white, so how are you to tell what sort of Duck's nest you have found? It is not so hard as it sounds, for a Duck's nest is always lined with the down from her own breast, and if whenever you pack a Duck's egg up you put in a few tufts of down from the nest, you can look it up in the book when you get home and find out for certain if you have got anything rare.

You won't often see the Drakes about the nest, but it is useful to know what they look like, for you will want to see what kind of fowl are on a lake, and with a good glass you can recognize them quite well. Then if you see something rare you won't mind spending a lot of time searching for the nest later on. They are rather hard to describe, so I advise you to study their pictures in a good book.

I.—THE MALLARD.
" Wild Duck " or " Grey Duck."

Bird.—This is the commonest of all, and you can study the Drake's colours in any farm-yard and the Duck's too; you will also notice that the Drake has the treble voice and the Duck the bass, and the wild ones are just the same.

Haunts.—Its haunts are lakes and rivers, and it is as fond of the moors as of the Fens, so you may come across it anywhere.

Nest.—The favourite place for a Grey Duck's nest is in long grass or rushes near the water's edge, but she is not particular, and I have heard of nests a long way from the water, and seen several in trees and bushes, and in hedge-bottoms too.

The nest is a hollow, lined with grass or whatever is to be found on the spot, and lots of down. The Duck sits tight, and when disturbed slips away without any fuss. Fuss generally means a brood of young ones somewhere near.

Eggs.—The eggs, green and smooth, are about 12, and if the bird is away you will find them covered up. All ducks do the same as far as I know.

Down.—The down is brownish-grey with just the tips white, and the tufts are big.

Season.—The laying season varies a great deal. April is the favourite month, but I have seen young Ducks swimming about in the first week of it, and have found eggs in May.

2.—THE TEAL.

Bird.—This is a little fellow, often called the "Half-Duck," rather tame, and very swift on the wing. The Drake is brightly-coloured, with a chestnut cheek-stripe and other points which you can see best in a picture. The Duck is like a small Wild Duck.

Haunts.—Teal haunt much the same places as Mallard, but are fonder of running water at most times of the year. I think in the North they nest more on the moors than on the low ground, and the nest is often a good distance from the water, in a tuft of heather or bent on one of the mosses, though it may be among the rushes near the loch or burn.

Nest.—The nest is the usual Duck nest, but the grass is often better built up, and the whole thing very snug. The bird sits close.

Eggs.—The eggs are creamy-coloured, and nine is about the average number.

Fig. 25.—Woodcock
(see page 178)

FIG. 26 – CORMORANTS

(see page 187)

Down.—The down is dark brown, and the tufts quite small.

Season.—They begin to lay about the 1st of May.

3.—THE SHOVELLER.

Bird.—This bird gets its name from its queer bill, which is very broad in front, and you will sometimes hear it called " Spoonbill " in the North. The Drake is a handsome, piebald-looking bird, chiefly chestnut-brown below. You might recognize him on the water by his dark green head, big black bill, and white breast and shoulder-patches. The Duck is the usual brown.

Haunts and Nest.—He is a rare bird, generally haunting a loch with a good fringe of rushes and sedge, and nesting on the ground among the same sort of cover as a Mallard would choose. The nest is much the same, a hollow with a little dry grass for a lining, and plenty of down of course.

Eggs.—The eggs are from eight to twelve, pale green, and rather smaller than a Mallard's.

Down.—The down is dark grey with pale centres and fairly good white tips. The tufts are a smaller size than the Mallard's.

Season.—May is soon enough to expect eggs.

4.—THE TUFTED DUCK.

Bird.—Smaller than a Mallard, with head, neck, breast and back black, a white patch on the wing, and all white below. He also has a crest which curls over towards his back. The Duck has very little crest and is brown above, lighter brown below. You meet them in pairs at any time of the year.

Haunts.—I think this Duck prefers the smaller lochs. but it is never very common. It nests in the usual sort of place, generally close to the water, and I have seen its eggs in an old Coot's nest.

Eggs.—The eggs are about nine, yellowish green and shiny.

Down.—The tufts are nearly black, with paler centres.

Season.—Any time from late April to early June.

5.—THE POCHARD.

Bird.—This bird is rare North of Yorkshire. You can tell it in the distance, swimming or flying, by its being dark at both ends and light in the middle. With a glass you may make out its bill, which is dark at both ends with a broad blue band round the middle.

Nest, Eggs and Down.—Its nest is generally near the water, often right in it, and the eggs are very like a Tufted Duck's, but the down-tufts are large, greyish-brown with dull white centres.

Season.—Some time in May.

6.—THE EIDER DUCK (Fig. 27).

Bird.—This is a big sea-duck, and the Drake is easily recognized by being light above and dark below, with a dark top to his head. The Duck is dark-brown, about the colour of dry seaweed.

Haunts.—It only nests on the Farnes in England, and in a good many parts of the Scottish coast, generally on an island.

Nest.—The nest is a big affair lined with a great mass of down, and is generally built among grass or weeds, which sometimes grow up round the sitting bird and hide her altogether.

Habits.—She never seems to leave the nest once she has started to sit, and will often let you stroke her without offering to move. She is often very hard to see.

Eggs; Season.—The eggs are generally six, green and far bigger than any other Duck's, and June is the best time for them.

These are all the Ducks that you are likely to meet with, but I will just mention the rest shortly.

7.—THE GADWALL.

Only known to breed in or near Norfolk. Nearly as big as a Mallard. Both Drake and Duck has a *white* wing-patch like a Tufted Duck, by which you can recognize them. Nest and eggs very like a Mallard's, and the down the same colour, but the tufts much smaller and the white tips almost invisible. Season, May.

8.—THE PINTAIL.

Only nests in a few places in Scotland and Ireland. Can be recognized by the two long feathers in its tail, and its extra long neck as well. Nests well away from the water. Eggs like a Mallard's. Down, sooty-brown with small white tips. Season, May.

9.—THE WIGEON.

Only in the North of Scotland. Known by the buff stripe along the top of his head, and his whistle of "Whee-you." Eggs creamy white and down sooty-brown with good white tips. Season, May.

10.—THE GARGANEY.

Only known on the Norfolk Broads in any numbers. Same size as a Teal, and has a strong white stripe over the eye. Nests in various places, often away from the water. Tufts of down, small, and brown with long white tips. Season, May.

11.—THE COMMON SCOTER.

Only in the far North of Scotland. A big black Duck, bigger than a Mallard. Nests on an island if it can. Down-tufts large, and brownish-grey with pale centres. Season, May.

12.—THE GOOSANDER.

In a few places in Scotland, but very rare. More the shape of a Cormorant than a Duck, black and white and as big as a Scoter. Nests in a hole in a tree for choice, or in a rock. Down, greyish-white. Season, April and May.

13.—THE RED-BREASTED MERGANSER.

Like the last bird, but with a wiry crest, part of which points backward, and part downward. Not uncommon in Scotland and Ireland. Nests among rocks, generally in a hole or crevice. Down in big tufts, pale brownish-grey, with centres and tips a little lighter. Season, May and June.

THE GULL TRIBE.

Contains three families:—
First, the true Gulls.
Second, the Terns, or Sea-swallows.
Third, the Petrels, which are really very different, but more like the Gulls than any other birds.

FAMILY XXIX.
THE GULLS.

There is no need to tell you what a Gull looks like. His beak tells you he is a robber by profession, and his long wings and webbed feet give you an idea of how he spends his spare time. You will notice that most Gulls have the same sort of plumage, " mantle " grey or black, and the rest white. (The Skuas are different in this, in fact they are the black sheep of the family in more ways than one).

They nest in colonies as a rule, either on the coast or inland, and build good solid nests when there is any need for it, though if a mere scrape will do as well, it is good enough for them.

Their eggs are all very much alike, and easy to recognize when you have seen a few. The favourite colour is very like a Curlew's, but the ground-colour especially varies from dark olive brown to pale blue, and that even in the same nest. It may be that they lay in each other's nests, as I have never seen these blue-coloured eggs except in big colonies. On the other hand I am told by one who has studied Richardson's Skua in the Shetlands that the first clutch of eggs laid by that bird are always brown, but if they are taken the second lot are blue. That looks as if the bird ran short of the brown colour quite suddenly, and the same bird might possibly lay two brown eggs and one blue one. If you are ever amongst Gulls when they begin to lay, you should notice if all the eggs at first are brown, and blue ones begin to turn up later after they have been robbed a bit.

The young ones are hatched with down on, but don't leave the nest in a hurry. Their first plumage is spotted with brown, and some of them take as much as four years to get their proper feathers.

THE SKUAS.

These are different from the rest of the Gulls in being dark all over and having hooked claws on their webbed feet. Some live in the Arctic, some in the Antarctic, but two of them, the Great Skua and Richardson's Skua, nest in the Shetlands. Their name comes from the cry they give, and they live by robbing other birds of the fish they catch, chasing them till they drop it. They both nest on moors or hillsides not far from the sea, and the nest is often only a scrape in the heather. The big one's eggs are as big as a Lesser Black-backed Gull's, and Richardson's about the size of a Black-headed Gull's, and you can make no mistake about the birds. Early June is the time for them.

I.—THE HERRING GULL.

Bird.—This is the big Gull with the silver-grey back which you see everywhere round the coast.

Haunts.—It nests in various places, on ledges of the cliffs, or on the ground on rocky islands. It very seldom comes inland to breed, but there is a big colony in Westmorland, and there may be others. I have seen odd pairs up the Tyne in Summer, but I never saw any sign that they had a nest.

Nest.—The nest may be big and solid, or practically nothing at all, according to where it is built. It is made chiefly of turf and seaweed, and lined with grass.

Eggs.—The two or three eggs are large, and the ground colour is often lightish brown, though it may be any of the standard Gull shades; the markings are spots rather than blotches, dark and light brown, and not too many of them.

Season.—June is the best month for them.

2.—THE LESSER BLACK-BACKED GULL.

Bird.—This is another very common Gull, and its name describes it very well, except that it is about as big as a Herring Gull.

Haunts and Nests.—It nests in big colonies, on the Farnes and in many parts of the Scottish coast, and also inland in some places, as at Hindley Steel in Northumberland. On the coast it prefers the level to the rock-ledges, and one of the Farnes is covered with their nests; on the moors they breed on a big open moss, most of the nests being just hollows in the heather.

Eggs.—The eggs run through the usual range of colours, and the markings may be blotches, spots, streaks, or all three at once. The size varies, too, but they are seldom quite as big as a Herring Gull's; three is the usual number.

Season.—They are laid early in May, though someone nearly always takes them for eating, so that you may be pretty sure of finding some eggs in June.

Habits.—These Gulls are about the worst thieves of the lot, and take eggs and young of Ducks and Grouse and any other birds they can find on the moor. Even lambs are not always safe from them, and they are said to peck out the eyes of a " cast " sheep if they find one. On the coast they rob the other sea-fowls' nests unmercifully. In Winter they bother the shore-shooter by pouncing on birds that fall in the water and gobbling them up before his eyes, so altogether they are a bad lot. Their only use is to act as scavengers to the fishing villages, cleaning up the fish refuse which, but for them, would spoil the effect of the sea-breezes altogether.

3.—THE BLACK-HEADED GULL.

Bird.—This is the smallest of the Gulls, with a dove-grey mantle, and (in Summer only) a head which looks black, but is really chocolate-brown.

Haunts.—These Gulls are very common, may be seen inland at all times of the year, and I think never breed by the sea. Their "gulleries" are common in the North, and some of them have many hundreds of nests. Most of them are in marshes at the heads of lakes, and though some are on mosses where there is no water but a small stream, I think they like to have open water near.

Nest.—The nests are built on the ground, quite big affairs in a wet place, but if they can find a good solid tussock they do little more than scratch out a hollow in the top of it.

Eggs.—The three eggs are much the same as the last bird's in colouring, and if possible *more* varied in size and markings, so that if you want a collection of all the varieties you need a big basket to bring them away in. They are the smallest of all Gulls' eggs.

Season.—Laying begins early in April sometimes, but usually someone collects the eggs and the birds keep on laying right into June.

Food.—This Gull does not rob other birds like the Black-back, but feeds on worms and insects, and often suffers from raids by Jackdaws and other robbers. At the end of June when the Ghostswift moths are out you will see lots of these Gulls hawking after them at dusk, miles away from their Gulleries.

4.—THE KITTIWAKE.

Bird.—This is another small Gull, very little bigger than the last, with a light-grey " mantle " and black legs. It cries out its own name, so you will need no introduction when you meet it.

Haunts.—It nests wherever there are high steep cliffs, as at Flamboro', the Farnes, St. Abb's Head, or the Bass. There are generally just about as many nests as there are suitable ledges, at any height from ten feet to the top, and you will not find many that are easy to get at.

Nest.—The nest is a good solid affair of turf, seaweed and grass, often looking like a bracket fixed to the rock, and both the nest and the rock below are all white with droppings.

Eggs.—The two or three eggs are often light brown, with the markings arranged in a ring, but they *may* be any colour that other Gulls' eggs are, so that there is really nothing but their size and the nest to distinguish them from others. They are hardly bigger than a Black-headed Gull's.

Season.—They generally have eggs before the end of May.

5.—THE COMMON GULL.

This is the rarest Gull, here, but its name means that it has a big range and is found in many parts of the world. It is not supposed to breed in England, but as it does so in Scotland and Ireland, and in scattered pairs as well as in colonies, there seems to be no reason why it should not turn up occasionally.

Bird.—It has a grey mantle, and is bigger than a Kittiwake, but much smaller than a Herring Gull, and its legs are yellow, not black, so that it should be easily recognized.

Nest, Etc.—It nests both on the coast and inland, on the ground as a rule, but sometimes on a rock-ledge. The eggs are said to be brown only, and the markings generally small spots; and in size they are rather bigger than a Kittiwake's, but much smaller than the big Gulls'.

6.—THE GREAT BLACK-BACKED GULL.

If you get close to one of these fellows he looks like a young Albatross, and you realise why the other one is called "Lesser." He is a bigger rogue than his young brother, if possible, and kills lambs quite easily.

He can be seen anywhere in Winter, but in Summer is much commoner in Scotland than in England, where he is said not to nest on the East Coast at all.

These Gulls do not often nest in colonies, but in single pairs, generally on the coast, but sometimes inland; more often on a ledge or the top of a rock than on the ground. They don't make much of a nest, and the eggs are said to be always of the brown type, with small spotty markings; and, of course, they are the biggest of all, so you ought to be able to identify a nest if you should have the luck to find one.

That is the last of the Gulls that breed with us, and the most interesting thing about their eggs is the way they vary. If any of you get the chance you should study them properly, and try to settle the question whether it is always the *same* bird that lays the blue type of egg, or whether one bird can lay *both* kinds.

FAMILY XXX.

The Terns, or Sea-Swallows.

These birds are very near relations of the Gulls, and have the same sort of habits, though their way of fishing is to hover a good height above the sea and plunge down like a hawk on their prey. They are smaller than the Gulls, and have a long forked tail like a Swallow's, and a thin, straight beak without the hook that the Gulls have.

They are much commoner in the Tropics than here, and all the five Terns that nest with us are Summer visitors, and you need not go to look for their eggs before June.

These five are all much the same colour, white, except for the pearl-grey mantle, and black top to the head. You distinguish them by the colour of beak and legs, and by their different sizes.

They nest in big colonies, very close together on the sand or shingle, and make very little nest or none at all. Two eggs is the usual number, and they are Gull colour and just about as variable as Gulls' eggs; so when the birds are about the same size you may find it hard to distinguish them. However, in a big colony you ought to be able to make sure which Tern it is, as all you need is a good look at one of them.

The young ones get out of the nest almost as soon as they are hatched, and stroll about the colony, and whether the mothers know their own or not I cannot say, but they all seem to get fed.

We will take the Terns in order of size, the biggest first.

1.—THE SANDWICH TERN.

Bird.—This one is nearly as big as a Kittiwake, and is often called " The Tern " on the coast, while the other kinds are just " Sea Swallows." It has a black bill and legs, and a loud cry, something like " kirhitt," which tells you when you are getting near the colony.

Haunts.—They nest at the Farnes on the East Coast, at Ravenglass on the West, and at a good many places further North.

Nest.—At the Farnes there is a colony on a low gravelly island. The nests are close together, scrapes in the shingle, with sometimes a little lining; and the eggs are so hard to see among the stones and so close together that it is almost impossible to avoid treading on them. In other places you may find them well above sea-level, and on various kinds of ground, but there is no difficulty in finding the spot, as the birds rise in a cloud and hover over their nests screaming all the time.

Eggs.—The eggs are generally two, sometimes three, the ground colour may be any shade from white to light brown, and the dark markings very handsome, but so varied that I can't attempt to describe them. Of course they are much bigger than the other Terns' eggs.

2.—THE COMMON TERN (Fig. 28).

Haunts.—This is the commonest Tern round the South of England, but not so common North of the Farnes, where there are a few.

Bird.—It is a good deal smaller than the last, but much the same colour. Its beak is red, *with a black tip*, and its legs red.

Nest.—This Tern prefers sand to gravel, and you will generally find its colonies among links or sand-hills, though probably on gravel at the Farnes. The nest is generally a mere scrape, but sometimes has quite a lot of lining.

Eggs.—It is no good trying to describe the eggs, as you will see for yourselves, but in shape they are generally rather round, and some shade of brown is the colour.

3.—THE ARCTIC TERN.

Bird.—This bird is very like the last, and looks just the same size, but it is really rather a smaller bird, with a longer tail to make up the difference. Its bill is *all red*.

Haunts.—It is the commonest Tern on the Farnes, rare further South, and commoner to the North, all the way to the Shetlands, where the Common Tern does not go at all. It likes islands better than the sandy stretches of coast of which the other is so fond.

Nest.—I don't think this Tern ever lines its nest, and the eggs are just as hard to see as the others. At the Farnes I was once standing admiring the Arctic Terns' nests all around me, when a bird swooped down out of the cloud hovering over us and hit me hard on the head; and she kept on doing this till I found I was standing with one foot in her nest, and took it out. That showed that each bird must know its own nest from above, which is rather wonderful when there are hundreds all alike and nearly touching one another; and it is just possible that they can recognize their own children among the crowds of young ones wandering about among the nests.

Eggs.—The eggs are slightly smaller than the Common Tern's, and longer in shape as a rule. Remember that the Common Tern is the rarer bird at the Farnes.

4.—THE ROSEATE TERN.

This is a very rare bird, but one or two pairs may breed at the Farnes or elsewhere. It comes between the last two in size, and as you can't distinguish between *them* by the eggs alone, the only way to be sure of this one is to watch the bird settle on her nest, which will probably be on the outskirts of a colony of the commoner sorts. The points you will know her by are these:
 1.—Bill black, and legs red.
 2.—Breast rosy (but the others are often salmon-pink).
 3.—Edges of the wing-quills white all the way to the tip.
 4.—Mantle slightly paler grey.

5.—THE LITTLE TERN.

Bird.—This is so much smaller than the rest that it is easily known, for it is no larger than a Thrush, and its eggs scarcely bigger. It is much the same colour as the others, but has a white forehead and yellow bill and legs.

Haunts.—You will find it at Ravenglass, but hardly at the Farnes, and it is generally commoner in the South than in the North, but not really common anywhere.

It nests in small colonies on the sands, preferring the mainland to an island, and I believe there are a few places where it breeds inland.

Eggs.—The two eggs (or perhaps three) are laid in a hollow in the sand, and are generally lighter in colour than the other Terns', so that they match the sand better and are even harder to see.

You may see the Black Tern in April or May, but though it used to nest in the Fens it has not done so for over 50 years, and those you see are just passing through; but if you should see them in June, well, it would be worth while having a look round, wouldn't it?

FAMILY XXXI.
THE PETRELS.

The Albatrosses are these birds' nearest relations, rather than the Gulls, and their distinguishing mark is the beak. Their nostrils end in a tube running about half-way along the top of it, which is easy enough to see when the bird is near you.

These birds are famous for following ships further away from land than any Gull goes, and they got their name from their habit of flying low over the water and paddling with their feet as they go; they look as if they were walking on the water, like St. Peter, so they were given the name of Petrel.

Four of them breed in our islands, chiefly on the West coasts of Scotland and Ireland, though the Storm Petrel has once been known to nest on the Bass Rock. Most of them nest in burrows, or holes in cliffs, and lay only one egg, which is white and chalky-looking, generally with a few small red spots round the big end. The smaller Petrels' eggs take five or six weeks to hatch, the big ones probably longer.

Most of them only fly about towards night, so you may be walking on top of their burrows and never know there are any about, but the holes have a strong musky smell.

1.—THE STORM PETREL.

The smallest of all, nearly black, with a white patch above the tail. The egg is about the size of a Thrush's, and is laid in June. In England a few breed in the Scilly Isles, Lundy, and a few places on the Welsh coast; it is much commoner on the Scotch and Irish coasts.

2.—LEACH'S FORK-TAILED PETREL.

Rather bigger than the last, and much the same colour, but with the forked tail. The egg is about the size of a big Missel-Thrush's, and is also laid in June. It breeds only in the Hebrides and St. Kilda, and on the Blaskets, off the Kerry coast.

3.—THE MANX SHEARWATER.

A big bird, black above, white below. Has rounded wings and glides over the water without flapping them. No longer nests on the Isle of Man, in spite of its name, but does so on the Scilly Isles and Lundy, and in many places in the Hebrides and Ireland. Egg as big as a Puffin's and laid in a burrow about the end of May.

4.—THE FULMAR PETREL.

Nearly as big as a Herring Gull, and much the same colour, but its rounded wings and flight are quite different. Only known to nest on St. Kilda, the Shetlands, and some of the Hebrides. These birds nest on sheltered ledges rather than in holes, and the islanders often snare them as they sit. Their laying time is from May to June.

THE PENGUIN TRIBE.

This is our last group of birds, and contains three families, all very clever in the water, but fearfully

Fig. 27 — Eider Ducks (sitting)

(see page 194)

Fig. 28—Terns
(see page 204)

FIG. 29 — GUILLEMOTS

(see page 209)

Fig. 30—Guillemots

(see page 209)

clumsy on land. Their bodies are so long and their feet set so far back that they are more like screw steamers than paddle-boats in the water, and on shore they can only sit up on their tails and waddle in a ridiculous fashion. The Penguins themselves only live in the Antarctic, but they show what a bird comes to that persists in swimming with its wings, for theirs are just like a Seal's flippers, and they can't fly at all. Our Great Auk had reached the same stage, and is now no more, as he was too easy to kill, and the fishermen cut the last of him up for bait years ago. The rest of them can fly, some of them very strongly, but none gracefully, and some have so little control that the only place they can *land* on is the *water*, so to speak.

FAMILY XXXII.
THE AUKS.

There is little more to say about this family, except that they spend 10 months out of the 12 at sea and only come ashore to breed, and as a rule lay only one egg, and not being able to sit on it, straddle over it and do their best to keep it warm that way. It seems to work all right, for plenty of young ones come out. These are covered with down, but quite helpless at first, and get down from the cliffs into the sea long before they can fly. I hope you may be there to see exactly how this is done. For all these birds the best month is June.

I.—THE GUILLEMOT (Figs. 29, 30).

" Marrot," " Willock " or " Scoot."

Haunts.—This is a common bird where there are cliffs, and at the Farnes you will see the tops of the rocks called the Pinnacles so thick with them that there is not standing room for one more. In spite of the crush they live very peaceably together, and a curious thing you will notice is that when one shouts they all shout in chorus.

Bird.—The bird is dingy brown on the back, wings, head and neck, and white underneath. His back view shows a pair of spots like a coachman's buttons (which are really the ends of two narrow bars on his wings) and many of them have a sort of bridle-mark on the face, a light streak running round the eye and back from it. The beak is narrow and pointed.

Nesting-place.—The Guillemot makes no nest, but lays its egg on the bare rock, generally on some narrow ledge of the cliff, though the top of a rock-stack is better; but by the time every Guillemot has found a place to stand there are very few places left, good or bad.

Egg.—The egg is long and pointed, so that if it starts rolling it will go in a circle and not roll over the cliff, but you will seldom see any number of Guillemots go off in a hurry without a few eggs being dislodged as they go, for besides being clumsy they generally sit with their faces to the cliff, so that they have to turn round to get away.

As to colour, it may not be quite true that no two are alike, but out of an average hundred I think it would be easier to pick 50 that were different than five that were alike. There is no fear of your mistaking them for anything but Razorbills', and I can tell you how to know *them* from any Guillemot's.

2.—THE RAZORBILL.

Bird.—This is a rather smaller bird, much the same colour as a Guillemot, but darker, and while the other bird's bill is thin and sharp like a dagger, this one's is flattened at the sides, deep from top to bottom, and hooked at the end. Thus it has got its name of Razorbill, or "Couter-neb," which means much the same. If you see one swimming amongst the Guillemots, you will know it by its cocked-up tail.

If you want to know what a Great Auk looked like, just imagine a Razorbill twice as big.

Haunts.—Razorbills breed pretty well everywhere where the Guillemots are, but are not nearly so common, and they prefer a ledge with a bit of shelter over it if they can get one, or a hole in the rocks.

Egg.—The single egg is rather shorter than a Guillemot's, and the colour may be anything from white to light brown, with rich dark brown or black markings, very like some kinds of Guillemots'. But you can always tell a Razorbill's egg, when blown, by looking through the hole against the light, when the inside is seen to be light green like a Peewit's. Only a deep green Guillemot's could *look* green inside, and a Razorbill's is never that colour at all.

3.—THE BLACK GUILLEMOT.

Not uncommon on the West of Scotland, round the Irish coast, and on the Isle of Man, but not found anywhere on the English coast.

It is a smaller bird again, dark all over except for a white patch on the wing, with a bill like a Guillemot's and red legs and feet.

It nests in holes and crevices even more than the Razorbill, and lays two eggs, much the same colour as that bird's, but no bigger than a Kittiwake's.

4.—THE PUFFIN (Fig. 31).
"Sea-Parrot."

Bird.—You cannot mistake him in Summer, for he has an enormous orange-red bill, like a false nose. But this nose has gained *him* the name of "Couter-neb," as well as the Razorbill, so you can't always tell which the fishermen may mean. He has a big white patch round the eye, too, which gives him an owlish look, so he is rather a remarkable bird.

He often sits up on his tail like the others, but he can stand on his toes and run too, like an ordinary bird.

Nest.—You should find Puffins almost wherever there are cliffs, but not south of Flamboro' on the East Coast; they nest in burrows in the sandy cliff-top, and no doubt the big beak is a sort of pick-axe provided for digging them. It comes in handy for other things, too, such as turning rabbits out of *their* burrows when he fancies a ready-made hole, or biting your hand if you stick it in when the lady is at home; so take a good thick glove with you when you start on a Puffin-hunt.

Egg.—At the end of the burrow is a rough sketch of a nest containing the one egg, which, when new-laid, is whitish, with a few faint markings of grey and pale brown, generally in a ring round the thick end. But most of the eggs you will get are so stained by the bird's wet feet and the sand that you can't see the real colour or the markings at all. You should keep a real dirty one for your collection, but a nail-brush and soap will bring the dirt off any that you want to clean.

When the breeding season is over the Puffins shed their false noses and clear off for the rest of the year. Nobody sees them, but they must spend the Winter somewhere well out at sea.

FAMILY XXXIII.
THE DIVERS.

These birds are rather like Guillemots with a longer neck and an even longer body. They are strong fliers when they are up, but are so unhandy that you may sometimes see one, trying to come down in a good-sized lake, overshoot it, and have to climb up and circle round to try again. When he gets there he doesn't seem to be able to check his speed at all, but hits the water with a tremendous splash, and a forced descent on land would certainly kill him.

They are sea-birds most of the year, but their breeding haunts are inland lakes and pools, where they spend nearly all their time in the water.

They only come ashore to nest, and about five yards from the water is far enough for them, for they cannot stand up and waddle like a Guillemot, but move on land the same way as they do in the water, pushing themselves along on their bellies as if they were swimming. Thus they make a channel or groove from the shore to the nest, which makes it pretty easy to find.

The eggs are two, very long and oval, like the birds, and dark olive brown with darker spots.

Only two Divers nest in the British Isles.

1.—THE RED-THROATED DIVER.

The smaller of the two. Not uncommon in the West of Scotland and the Islands.

2.—THE BLACK-THROATED DIVER.

Much rarer, but breeding within much the same limits.

The second bird's eggs should be over three inches long, the first's under, but they vary; and if you should find eggs just about three inches long there may be some doubt about them. The birds will be swimming about, and besides their throats you should look at their backs. No. 1 is all brown and No. 2 black, spotted with white. No. 1 is said to breed on the shore as a rule; and No. 2 to prefer an island.

FAMILY XXXIV.
THE GREBES (Fig. 32).

The Grebes are very like the Divers, with long, boat-shaped bodies, and long, snaky necks, and their feet are almost as far back, though they can sit up on land when they want to. The reason I have made a separate family of them is that instead of having webbed feet like the rest, they have lobes of skin down the sides of the toes, like the Coot and the Phalarope. They nest in the water, and unlike any other bird I know, make no attempt to keep their eggs dry, and their eggs are the only ones I know to which the water-test doesn't apply —for even when a Grebe's egg is nearly hatched, it floats no higher above the water than a sponge does.

I.—THE LITTLE GREBE.
" Dabchick," " Ducker " or " Diver."

Bird.—This bird is dark brown above and rather lighter below, with some chestnut about the cheeks; and you can tell it from the Water-hens that are sure to be swimming about by its snaky head and neck, and its having no white under the tail. You cannot mistake its trick of diving, taking a header with a little splash, which has earned it the name of " Ducker," and you may see one doing its submarine trick of submerging gradually till only its beak is on the surface. It will stay there for some time, with nothing to hold on by, and apparently no paddling with the feet; but I suppose it must do something of the sort, for all birds are much too buoyant to stay under water without a big effort.

Cry.—Dabchicks have a peculiar long-drawn twittering cry, which reminds you of the scream of a Hawk, and is also a little like a horse neighing. You will hear this most in the early Spring before they have begun to build.

Haunts.—It is quite a common bird on suitable ponds, with plenty of weed, and also haunts slow-running rivers with good cover at the edges; but it needs a good deal more water than will satisfy a Water-hen, so you may easily have to go some distance to find a nest.

Nest.—Its nest is a heap of green weeds which the birds pull up from the bottom, and keep piling up till the mass floats within an inch or two above the water. If the water is very shallow the nest will rest on the bottom before there is enough of it to show much above the surface, but the process is the same either way; I have known a floating nest in the middle of a pond to be blown ashore by a big wind and stranded in quite shallow water—just right for photographing.

The top of the pile is hollowed out a little for the eggs, but not lined with anything to keep them dry.

Habits.—If the nest is at all open, you will see the bird sitting on it, but as you approach she gets very busy, dabbing her bill over the side and pulling up bits of weed which she spreads over the eggs. It is done in no time, and then over she goes and is seen no more. The nest now looks like a wet heap of rubbish, and many an egg-stealer, human or other, must have been taken in by this trick. It looks so natural that even when I have seen the bird do it I sometimes feel a sort of shock of surprise when I pull off the covering and see the eggs.

Eggs.—They are generally five, pointed at both ends and pure white when laid, but they soon get stained brown by their wet bed, and you can judge how hard sat they are by their colour, as the water test is no good.

Young.—They take three weeks to hatch, and the young ones take to the water at once. If you disturb a brood of them out in the open you may be lucky enough to see the old ones tuck the chicks on their backs and swim off to shelter with them; and I have heard that when they are badly scared they will even dive with the young ones sticking tight all the time.

Season.—The time of laying varies according to the cover that can be got, and early in May is generally soon enough to look for eggs. If the first lot are not too late, there will generally be a second brood about the beginning of July, and if you see a fleet of young ones by themselves, or with only one parent, there is very likely a new brood under way already. Of course second nests will be much better hidden and harder to find.

2.—THE GREAT CRESTED GREBE.

This is still a rare bird, but is increasing, and already breeds in one or two places in the North.

Bird.—It is a good deal bigger than the last, and can be recognized by its long body and long neck, which it generally holds straight up when swimming; but its most striking points are a crest like a pair of ears laid back, and a ruff of a bright chestnut tint which surrounds its face rather like a Cobra's hood.

Haunts.—Its haunts are bigger sheets of water with plenty of reeds and other cover, and if you are lucky enough to have a pair settle near you you ought to see them swimming about any time from the end of March.

If they should seem to disappear later, don't be too sure they have left the lake, for they often keep well out of sight after the nest is built.

Nest.—The nest is the same sort of affair as the Dabchick's, bigger and flatter, and generally well hidden away among the reeds, to which it is often anchored. There are often a few " sham " nests not far from the real one, so if you find one of these keep on hunting.

The bird covers her eggs in the same way as the Dabchick, but not always so cleverly, for you can often see the eggs showing through.

Eggs.—The eggs are generally four, much the same as the Dabchick's, but larger. You have to be there pretty soon after they are laid if you want a clean specimen.

Young.—The young ones are striped down the back with black and pale yellow, and have a bright red patch of bare skin on the head. The old birds often take them on their backs or give them a tow when in a hurry.

Season.—The time of laying varies from the end of April to June, according to what cover there is, and I expect if they get started in good time they will have a second brood, though I have never heard of one.

Two other Grebes are supposed to have nested in Britain, but I think if you see them it will be quite easy to find their nests first and their names afterwards —and I hope you will. They are just like the other two in their ways.

OBSERVATION.

That brings us to the end of the birds that nest in Britain, and I have tried to give you some useful information about each, and especially how to know the birds themselves; for if you are thinking of nothing but *nests* when you go out, you will find lots of common ones and miss most of the rare ones, simply through not noticing the birds.

Now supposing you are not a very observant person by nature, but would like to be, I can tell you how to manage it. It's quite simple, and just a question of habit. All you have to do is to get into the habit of naming every bird you see, just as you greet your friends when you meet them. You can leave out the " good-morning " and say to yourself " Yellowhammer," " Pied Wagtail " or whatever it may be; and when you see one you can't put a name to, get a real good look at him, and notice all you can about him—and if there is no-one on the spot who can tell you his name, look him up when you get home. There is an index in this book which will tell you which birds have any of the points you have noticed about him, such as white feathers in the tail, or bars on the wing, or a black throat or anything like that. If you haven't got enough points to make sure what he is, you will probably only have two or three left to choose from, and you can look them up easily enough either here or in a book with good pictures, or both; and then you ought to be able to make up your mind about him, and give him his right name next time you meet and ever afterwards.

If you only knew a few to start with, it makes it all the more interesting, and your circle of friends will get bigger every day.

If you've read even a little of this book you will have

discovered that lots of birds can be known by their voices better than by their looks, and you may think learning them is a hopeless job. It isn't. You can set about it in the very same way.

Start in March when there aren't too many at it, and just say to yourself whenever you hear one, "Chaffinch," "Hedge-Sparrow" or whatever it is. When you hear one that you don't know, and have no-one to ask, try to get a look at that bird. If you fail, you've got that note in your head and it won't be long before you *can* put a name to it.

Keep it up for a month, and you'll find yourself walking along, talking hard about aeroplanes or electricity and every now and then saying to yourself "Chiff-Chaff," "Great Tit," and so on, and not interrupting the conversation till the inner voice says "What's that bird?" and then the aeroplanes have to wait a minute till you find out. You've got the habit of noticing all the common sounds, and a new note is bound to catch your ear. When all the summer birds are here there is a regular chorus going on, and you won't learn all their songs in one season; but with the habit of noticing all you can, you will learn an astonishing lot, and it won't be long before a song you don't know means an egg you haven't got, and *that's* a useful hint at any rate.

And it's not only useful knowledge that you will get this way, but pleasure, too. I mean pleasure in the sounds themselves. I don't know whether you know anything about flowers. If you don't, you probably pass by scores of beautiful things in summer and never even notice them—at least that is how it used to be with me, till I got to know their names and all about them. Well, it's just the same with the songs of birds. The better you know them the better you like them, and you get endless pleasure out of sounds that lots of people never even *hear*.

HAUNTS.

So much for the habit of using your eyes and ears all the time. Now I am going to give you a list of the birds you may find in various places, so that when you know you are going to a moor or a marsh or a wood, you can look through the list for that particular sort of place, and, if you see any birds in it that you don't know, look them up, and find out how to know them and whether it is time for their nests yet, and if so, all about the nest and how to find it. I have left out some of the very commonest birds, and marked with a * some of the very rare ones, and those which only nest in a few places; and I have said nothing about the regular sea fowl, like Gulls and Guillemots.

1.—BIRDS OF THE MOORS.

Grouse (p. 147).
Golden Plover (p. 169).
Ring Ousel (p. 76).
Meadow Pipit (p. 50).
*Short-eared Owl (p. 139).
Blackgame (p. 149).
Merlin (p. 132).
Dunlin (p. 171).
Wheatear (p. 80).
*Dotterel (p. 172).
Curlew (p. 177).
Twite (p. 66).
Snipe (p. 180).
Nightjar (p. 127).
*Hen Harrier (p. 130).

2.—BIRDS OF THE WOODS.
Nests in trees.

Heron (p. 184).
Carrion Crow (p. 35).
Magpie (p. 40).
Jay (p. 42).
Horned Owl (p. 138).
Sparrow Hawk (p. 131).
Kestrel (p. 134).
*Hobby (p. 133).
Turtle Dove (p. 145).
Missel Thrush (p. 74).
*Hawfinch (p. 58).
Bullfinch (p. 59).
*Crossbill (p. 57).
*Siskin (p. 65).
Goldcrest (p. 115).

HAUNTS. 221

Holes in trees.

Brown Owl (p. 137).
*Woodpeckers (p. 118).
*Nuthatch (p. 117).
Tree-creeper (p. 116).
*Gooseander (p. 196).
*Pied Flycatcher (p. 103).

Nests on the ground.

*Wood Wren (p. 88).
*Nightingale (p. 78).
Woodcock (p. 178).
*Blackgame (p. 149).
*Capercaillie (p. 157).
Nightjar (open spaces) (p. 127).

Nests in the undergrowth.

Chiffchaff (p. 86).
*Lesser White Throat (p. 91).
Garden Warbler (p. 92).
Blackcap (p. 93).

3.—BIRDS OF THE RIVERSIDE.

Sandpiper (p. 174).
Grey Wagtail (p. 53).
Kingfisher (p. 122).
Sedge Warbler (p. 95).
*Oyster Catcher (p. 173).
Dipper (p. 98).
Yellow Wagtail (p. 55).
Sand Martin (p. 106).
Redshank (p. 175).
*Ringed Plover (p. 173).

4.—BIRDS OF THE MARSH.

Snipe (p. 180).
Water Rail (p. 159).
*Montagu's Harrier (p. 130).
Redshank (p. 175).
Meadow Pipit (p. 50).
*Marsh Harrier (p. 130).

5.—BIRDS OF THE LAKE.

Nests in the water.

Little Grebe (p. 214).
*Great Crested Grebe (p. 216).
Coot (p. 164).
Waterhen (p. 162).
*Spotted Crake (p. 161).
*Pochard (p. 194).
*Reed Warbler (over the water) (p. 94).

Nests on shore.

Reed Bunting (p. 70).
Ducks in general (p. 190).
Sedge Warbler (p. 95).
*Marsh Warbler (p. 95). and

Marsh birds (4).
*Divers (p. 213).
*Red-necked Phalarope (p. 183).
*Bearded Tit (p. 114).

6.—BIRDS OF THE ROCKS.

*Raven (p. 43).
*Buzzard (p. 129).
Jackdaw (p. 39).
*Peregrine (p. 132).

Kestrel (p. 134).
Stockdove (p. 144).
Swift (p. 126).

7.—BIRDS OF THE GORSE.

Linnet (p. 65).
*Cirl Bunting (p. 72).

Stonechat (p. 83).
*Dartford Warbler (p. 97).

8.—BIRDS OF THE ORCHARD.

*Goldfinch (p. 64).
*Hawfinch (p. 58).

9.—BIRDS OF THE FIELDS.

Corn Bunting (p. 69).
Skylark (p. 46).

Corn Crake (p. 158).
*Quail (p. 155).

10.—BIRDS THAT HAUNT BUILDINGS.

Barn Owl (p. 136).
Swallow (p. 104).

Swift (p. 126).
House Martin (p. 105).

11.—BIRDS OF THE SEA COAST (other than regular sea-fowl).

Rock Pipit (p. 51).
*Chough (p. 44).
*Rock Dove (p. 145).
Ringed Plover (p. 173).

Oyster Catcher (p. 173).
*Hooded Crow (p. 44).
*Peregrine (p. 132).

12.—BIRDS OF ALMOST ANYWHERE.

Redpoll (p. 67).
Tree Pipit (p. 49).
Coal Tit (p. 112).
*Grasshopper Warbler (p. 96).
Redstart (p. 79).
Spotted Flycatcher (p. 102).
Pied Wagtail (p. 52).
Great Tit (p. 113).
Long-tailed Tit (p. 109).
Willow Wren (p. 85).
Whinchat (p. 81).
Cuckoo (p. 120).
*Tree Sparrow (p. 61).
Blue Tit (p. 111).
Marsh Tit (p. 112).
Whitethroat (p. 90).
Wren (p. 99).

End of Part II.

PART III.
A BIRDSNESTING CALENDAR.

This gives the earliest dates on which some of the commoner birds have begun to lay, as shown by records kept at Corchester School since 1903. The order in which they come should be a fair guide in any year, but I have marked with a * any that seem to be rather late dates, even for the North; and these birds you may expect to find a little sooner.

Date.	Bird.	Date.	Bird.
March 12	Rook.	March 27	Woodpigeon.
17	*Heron.	31	Peewit.
19	Dipper.	April 2	Hedge Sparrow.
20	Thrush.		
22	Brown Owl.	4	Robin.
23	Blackbird.		Snipe (early).
27	Missel Thrush.	9	Carrion Crow.

Date.		Bird.	Date.		Bird.
April	10	Waterhen.	May	7	Coal Tit.
	11	Wild Duck.		8	Partridge.
	14	Magpie.		10	Tree Pipit.
		Long-eared Owl.		11	Little Grebe.
	15	Black-headed Gull.		12	Wheatear. Redpoll.
	16	Redshank. Pheasant.		13	Willow Wren.
	19	Greenfinch.		14	Lesser Whitethroat.
	20	Grey Wagtail.			*Sparrow Hawk.
	23	Starling. Curlew. Grouse.		15	Kingfisher. Linnet. Whitethroat.
	24	Jackdaw.			*Sand Martin.
	27	Pied Wagtail.			*Blackgame.
				16	Sandpiper.
	28	Long-tailed Tit. Goldcrest.		17	Swallow.
				24	Whinchat. Redstart.
	29	Golden Plover.		25	Spotted Flycatcher.
May	3	Wren. Blue Tit.		26	*Coot. Cuckoo.
	4	*Sparrow. Yellow-hammer. Kestrel. Meadow Pipit.		27	Corn Crake. Garden Warbler.
				31	Blackcap.
			June	1	Wood Wren.
				2	Sedge Warbler.
	5	*Skylark. Great Tit.		3	House Martin.
	7	*Chaffinch.			

FIG. 31—PUFFINS.
(see page 212)

FIG. 32—LITTLE GREBE
(see page 214)

CALENDAR.

Just a few pieces of advice on how to use this calendar.

First, If you live in the North you mustn't expect to find eggs on these dates, except in a very early year. In an average year the birds should begin some days later, and you are likely to *find* most of them a week after that, when they will have begun to sit. In the South, where things are much earlier, you may take these dates as the times when you ought to find them sitting. In both places you will find the order in which they come holds good fairly well, so that you can expect a rare bird to be nesting about the time when its commoner neighbours in the list are all at it.

For example, suppose you have to make a bit of a journey to find a Linnet's nest or a Sandpiper's—look at the list and you will see that Whitethroats begin about the same time and obviously the time to go is not such and such a day in May, but just whenever you begin to find lots of Whitethroats with eggs. It may be a bad year for Whitethroats (as sometime happens); then take the next common bird, the Swallow. If you go when most of them have eggs you won't be far wrong.

Another thing you should remember is that these are only the birds that we have found pretty regularly in one district; with none of the real South-country birds in the list; and there are a good many that breed regularly with us, which we don't find often enough to be able to say just when they begin. These are Woodcock, Jay, Pied Flycatcher, Chiff-Chaff, Swift, Nightjar and a good many more. Again there are North-country birds that we don't find at all, such as Ring-ousels, Dunlins, Reed Buntings and so on; and birds that turn up once in ten years or so, like Corn Buntings and Grasshopper Warblers. So wherever you live I advise you to make a calendar of your own, and let this one be just a rough guide as far as it goes, and not the last word on the subject.

I think you must see by this time what a great help it will be to keep a record of the time when you find not only the rare birds' nests but the common ones as well.

PART IV.
COLOUR INDEX.

Giving most of the points you are likely to notice about birds, and intended to help you to find out what they are. I have left out such as are very easy to recognize, like Peewits, or Herons.

I.—THE HEAD.

1. *With a crest.*

Skylark (p. 47).
Shag, (p. 187).
Jay (p. 42).
Crested Tit (p. 114).
Tufted Duck (p. 193).
Great Crested Grebe (p. 216).
Merganser (p. 196).

2. *Black all over.*

Reed Bunting (p. 70).
Black-headed Gull (Brown) (p. 200).

3. *Nearly all black.*

Tree Sparrow (p. 61).
Marsh Tit (p. 112).
Stonechat (p. 83).
Great Tit (p. 113).
Coal Tit (p. 112).

4. *Just the top black.*

Bullfinch (p. 59).
Blackcap (p. 93).
All the Terns (pp. 203-207).
Eider Drake (p. 194).

5. Red on top.

Linnet (p. 65).
Redpoll (p. 67).

Green Woodpecker (p. 119).

6. A black mask across the eyes.

Wheatear (p. 80).
Nuthatch (p. 117).
Red-backed Shrike (cock) (p. 108).

Ringed Plover (p. 173).
Redstart (cock) (throat and cheeks too) (p. 79).

7. A white forehead.

Redstart (cock) (p. 79).
Pied Flycatcher (p. 103).
Pied Wagtail (p. 52).

Wheatear (p. 80).
Ringed Plover (p. 173).
Little Tern (p. 206).

8. A white streak over the eye.

Whinchat (p. 81).
Wheatear (p. 80).
Tree-creeper (p. 116).
Blue-headed Wagtail (p. 55).
Dotterel (p. 172).

Dunlin (p. 171).
Garganey Drake (p. 196).
Meadow Pipit (faint) (p. 50).

9. A yellow streak over the eye.

Siskin (p. 65).
Skylark (p. 47).
Tree Pipit (p. 49).
Yellow Wagtail (p. 55).
Redwing (Thrush) (p. 75).
Chiff-chaff (pale) (p. 86).
Willow Wren (stronger) (p. 85).

Wood Wren (bright) (p. 88).
Garden Warbler (very faint) (p. 92).
Reed Warbler (pale) (p. 94).
Sedge Warbler (broad nearly white) (p. 95).

10. *White cheek-patches.*

All the common Tits (pp. 108 foll.).
Pied Wagtail (p. 52).
Goldfinch (p. 64).
House Sparrow (grey) (p. 60).
Tree Sparrow (with dark centre) (p. 61).
Stonechat (more on neck than cheeks) (p. 83).
Puffin (p. 212).
Cormorant (really across the throat) (p. 186).

II.—THE THROAT OR CHIN.

1. *Black.*

House Sparrow (cock) p. 60).
Tree Sparrow (p. 61).
Reed Bunting (p. 70).
Cirl Bunting (p. 72).
Hawfinch (p. 58).
Grey Wagtail (cock) (p. 53).
Pied Wagtail (p. 52).
Tits (p. 108).
Siskin (chin only) (p. 65).
Redpoll (chin only) (p. 67).

2. *White.*

Blackcap (p. 93).
Nuthatch (p. 117).
Whitethroat (p. 90).
Lesser Whitethroat (p. 91).
Sedge Warbler (p. 95).
Long-tailed Tit (p. 109).
Tree Pipit (p. 49).
Swift (p. 126).

3. *Speckled,* as it shows when the bird is on the nest.

Thrushes (pp. 72-74).
Blackbird (p. 75).
Ring Ousel (p. 76).
Meadow Pipit (p. 50).
Spotted Flycatcher (p. 102).
Grasshopper Warbler (p. 96).
Corn Bunting (p. 69).
Linnet (p. 65).

III.—THE WINGS.

1. *With two white bars.*

Tree Sparrow (p. 61).
Chaffinch (p. 63).
Coal Tit (p. 112).
Tree Creeper (faint) (p. 116).
Stone Curlew (p. 166).

2. *With one white bar.*

House Sparrow (p. 60).
Hawfinch (two when wing is spread) (p. 58).
Bullfinch (broad) (p. 59).
Great Tit (p. 113).
Blue Tit (p. 111).
Sandpiper (p. 174).
Dunlin (p. 171).
Ringed Plover (p. 173).
Phalarope (p. 183).
Oyster-catcher (broad) (p. 173).
Black Guillemot (broad) (p. 211).
Razorbill (narrow) (p. 210).
Coot (narrow) (p. 164).
Woodpigeon (broad) (p. 142).

3. *With white patches.*

Stonechat (p. 83).
Whinchat (p. 81).
Pied Flycatcher (p. 103).
Redshank (p. 175).
Eared Grebe (p. 217).
Nightjar (cock) (small ticks) (p. 127).
Tufted Duck (p. 193).
Gadwall (p. 195).

(Most Ducks have a wing-patch blue or green with white edges.)

4. *Barred with other colours.*

Goldfinch (1 broad yellow) (p. 64).
Goldcrest (1 black between 2 pale) (p. 115).
Rock Dove (2 black) (p. 145).
Redpoll (buff) (p. 67).
Corn Bunting (buff) (p. 69).

IV.—THE BACK.

1. *With a white patch on the rump.*

Jay (p. 42).
Wheatear (p. 80).
Stonechat (cock) (p. 83).
Curlew (p. 177).
2 Petrels (p. 207).
Hen Harrier (p. 130).
Bullfinch (p. 59).
House Martin (p. 105).
Redshank (p. 175).
Whimbrel (p. 182).
Rockdove (p. 145).

2. *With the rump lighter than the rest.*

Hawfinch (light brown) (p. 58).
Greenfinch (cock) (yellow) (p. 61).
Siskin (cock) (yellow) (p. 65).
Green Woodpecker (yellow) (p. 119).
Kingfisher (blue) (p. 122).
Red-backed Shrike (cock) (blue-grey) (p. 108).
Fieldfare (blue-grey) (p. 75).

3. *With a blue back.*

Most of the cock Hawks.
Cuckoo (p. 120).
Kingfisher (p. 122).
Nuthatch (p. 117).
Woodpigeon (p. 142).
Stockdove (p. 144).

V.—THE TAIL.

1. *With the outer feathers white.*

Skylark (p. 47).
All Wagtails and Pipits except Rock Pipit (grey) (pp. 49-56).
Great Tit (p. 113).
Long-tailed Tit (p. 109).
Chaffinch (p. 63).
Yellowhammer (p. 68).

2. *Outer feathers edged with white.*

Whitethroat (p. 90).
Lesser Whitethroat (p. 91).
Dartford Warbler (p. 97).

Linnet (p. 65).
Twite (very little) (p. 66).

Reed Bunting (p. 70).
Nuthatch (patches) (p. 117).

3. *Others showing white in the tail.*

Wheatear (base) (p. 80).
Whinchat (base) (p. 81).
Red-backed Shrike (base) (p. 108).
Goldfinch (centre) (p. 64).
Sandpiper (tips and sides) (p. 174).

Hawfinch (tips) (p. 58).
Turtle Dove (tips) (p. 145).
Snipe (p. 180).
Waterhen (underneath) (p. 162).
Blackcock (underneath) (p. 149).

4. *Birds showing yellow in the tail.*

Greenfinch (p. 61).
Siskin (p. 65).

Wood Wren (sometimes) (p. 88).

5. *Birds with a barred tail.*

Wryneck (p. 119).
Most Hawks and Owls.
Nightjar (p. 127).
Woodcock (p. 178).

Snipe (p. 180).
and many with very short tails like Sandpipers. Redshanks, etc.

6. *Birds with an extra long tail for their family.*

Magpie
Long-tailed Tit
Dartford Warbler
Twite
Grey Wagtail
Wryneck
Turtle Dove
Pintail

(Crows).
(Tits).
(Warblers).
(Finches).
(Wagtails).
(Woodpeckers).
(Pigeons).
(Ducks).

VI.—THE BREAST.

1. *Birds with the breast black.*

Golden Plover (chin to tail) (p. 169).
Dunlin (middle part) (p. 171).
Eider Drake (crop to tail) (p. 194).
Dotterel (belly only, breast chestnut) (p. 172).

(The rest of this section deals with small birds only.)

2. *Breast red.*

Linnet (cock) (p. 65).
Redpoll (cock) (p. 67).
Bullfinch (cock) (p. 59).
Crossbill (cock) (p. 57).

3. *Breast brownish-red.*

Stonechat (throat black) (p. 83).
Redstart (cock) (throat black) (p. 79).
Dartford Warbler (p. 97).
Kingfisher (throat white) (p. 122).

4. *Breast rosy-pink.*

Chaffinch (p. 63).
Red-backed Shrike (cock) (p. 108).

5. *Breast orange.*

Nuthatch (p. 117).
Bearded Tit (p. 114).

6. *Breast pale salmon pink.*

Long-tailed Tit (throat white) (p. 109).
Whinchat (p. 81).

7. *Breast yellow, chin to tail.*

Yellow Wagtail (p. 55).
Blue-headed Wagtail (p. 55).
Grey Wagtail (hen) (p. 53).
Greenfinch (cock) (p. 61).
Crossbill (hen) (p. 57).

8. *Breast mostly yellow.*

Great Tit (with a black stripe) (p. 113).
Blue Tit (with a blue stripe) (p. 111).
Grey Wagtail (cock) (with a black throat) (p. 53).
Wood Wren (upper part) (p. 88).
Siskin (streaked) (p. 65).
Yellowhammer (streaked) (p. 68).

9. *Breast pure white, chin to tail.*

Tree Creeper (p. 116).
Pied Flycatcher (p. 103).
House Martin (p. 105).

NOTE.—Most small birds are greyish or yellowish below, not pure white.

10. *Breast speckled.*

Thrush (spotted all over).
Missel Thrush (spotted all over).
Fieldfare (spotted on throat and flanks).
Redwing (spotted on throat and flanks).
Linnet (hen) (all over) (p. 65).
Twite (hen) (all over) (p. 66).
Pipits (upper breast and flanks) (pp. 49-51).
Skylark (upper breast) (p. 47).
Grasshopper Warbler (upper breast) (p. 96).
Spotted Flycatcher (upper breast faint) (p. 102).

11. *Breast barred.*

Wryneck (the whole) (p. 119).
Cuckoo (all but the throat) (p. 120).
Red-backed Shrike (hen) (p. 108).
Sparrow-hawk (p. 131).
Woodcock (p. 178).

VII.—THE WHOLE BIRD.

1. *Birds that look black-and-white.*

Magpie (p. 40).
Oyster Catcher (p. 173).
Spotted Woodpeckers (both) (p. 119).
Pied Flycatcher (p. 103).
Pied Wagtail (p. 52).

Eider Drake (p. 194).
Sheldrake (both) (p. 189).
Shoveller Drake (p. 193).
Goosander (p. 196).
Merganser (p. 196).

2. *Birds that look yellow.*

Green Woodpecker (p. 119).
Greenfinch (p. 61).
Siskin (p. 65).
Yellowhammer (p. 68).
Wood Wren (p. 88).

Yellow Wagtail (p. 55).
Blue-headed Wagtail (p. 55).
Grey Wagtail (sometimes) (p. 53).

That is the end of the Index, not because there is nothing more to say about the look of birds, but because if it gets any bigger you'll never use it.

Now I had better give you an idea of how to use it. Suppose you have seen a stumpy little bird with a very slight tinge of pink on the breast and a white streak over the eye; you turn up the breast section, and see this: "6. Breast pale salmon pink. Long-tailed Tit and Whinchat." You know him now, for he certainly had not a long tail, but to make sure you turn to the head, and see: "8. A white streak over the eye." The first bird you see is Whinchat, so now you have no doubt about him, and if you look him up in his proper place, you will find when, where and how he nests and the best way to find him.

Again, suppose you have seen a yellow-looking little bird building its nest on the ground, you will turn up:

VII.—The Whole Bird, and there you will find the birds that look Yellow. It wasn't a Woodpecker and you know a Greenfinch, a Yellowhammer and a Wagtail by sight. So you are left with two, Siskin and Wood Wren. You look up Siskin first, and find it builds in fir-trees— and if you go to that nest later on and it doesn't agree with my account of a Wood Wren's, well, something must be wrong with the book or your eyes, that's all.

MYSTERIES.

Now I have told you all I think you want to know to give you a good start as birdsnesters, and I hope you'll get as much fun out of it as I have. I will finish up with a few questions, and if you can answer them all by the time you're as old as I am you'll have done pretty well; but I bet you'll be asking yourselves some more, and harder ones, by that time. For there's no man alive that knows all about birds, nor ever will be.

Why are some eggs coloured, and some plain, and can you find a reason for the different markings?

Why should Sparrow Hawks, Buzzards and Eagles have a good idea of building a nest, and the Falcons none at all?

How does a rare bird like a Peregrine or a Raven, who loses his mate in the nesting season, find another to take charge of the eggs before they are cold?

How does a Corncrake, which doesn't seem to be able to fly 100 yards, and can be caught on the wing by a dog, manage to get to Africa for the winter?

What makes young birds push off on their autumn migration while the old ones are still here, moulting, and how do they find their way?

Does a Guillemot know its own egg amongst the crowd, and can that be why no two are alike?

Is it always birds that nest in colonies that have so many varieties of eggs, or are there any exceptions?

How many eggs does one Cuckoo lay, and are they all the same colour?

How did Woodpigeons get so common, only laying 2 eggs at a time? and what becomes of all the young Tits? (Two broods of 8-12 every summer.)

Whatever makes a Nightingale sing at night?

Why do Wagtails do it? and are their long tails any *use* to them?

Why should the hen hawk always be so much bigger than the cock?

Can any birds sleep on the wing, and, if so, which?

How does a Grebe submerge like a submarine?

Are the Sparrows that nest in your ivy the same that roost there in winter? Give reasons for your answer.

There are plenty more like this, but I think those are enough for the present.

THE END.

GENERAL INDEX.

"Apple-shealer," 63.
Auks, 209.
Baillon's Crake, 162
"Bank Lark," 49.
"Bank Martin," 106.
Barn Owl, 136.
Bearded Tit, 114.
Bell-cute and Bellpoot, 164.
Birds of Prey, 128-141.
Bittern, 185.
Black backed Gull, Lesser, 199.
Black-backed Gull, Greater, 202.
Blackbird, 75.
Blackcap, 93.
Blackcock, 149.
Blackgame, 149.
Black Grouse, 149.
Black Guillemot, 211.
"Black-headed Bunting," 70.
Black-headed Gull, 200.
"Black Martin," 126.
Black-throated Diver, 213.
"Blue-cap," 111.
"Blue Hawk," 132.
Blue-headed Wagtail, 55.
Blue Tit, 111.
"Bottle Tit," 109.
"Brown Linnet," 65.
Brown Owl, 137.
Bullfinch, 59
Buntings, 68-72.
"Butcher-bird," 108.
Buzzard, 129.
Capercaillie, 157.
Carrion Crow, 35.
Castings, 141.
Chaffinch, 63.
"Chats," 79-83.
Chiff-chaff, 86.
"Chitter-chat," 95.
Chough, 44.
Cirl Bunting, 72.

Coal Tit, 112.
Common Bunting, 69.
Coot, 164.
"Corbie," 35.
Cormorants, 186
Corn Bunting, 69.
Corncrake, 158.
"Couter-neb," 210 or 212.
"Crane," 184.
Crested Tit, 114.
Crossbill, 57.
Crow Family, 35-44.
Cuckoo, 120.
Curlew, 177.
"Cushat," 142.
"Dabchick," 214.
Dartford Warbler, 97
Dipper, 98.
"Diver" (local name), 214.
Divers, 213.
"Dooker" or "Ducker," 214.
Dotterel, 172.
Doves, 142-146.
Ducks, 190-196.
Dunlin, 171.
Eagles, 128.
Eider Duck, 194.
Falcons, 132-135.
"Feather Poke," 85, 88.
"Fern Owl," 127.
Fieldfare, 75.
Finches, 56-72.
"Fire-tail," 79.
Flycatchers, 102-104.
Fork-tailed Petrel, 208
"Frenchman," 156.
Fulmar Petrel, 208.
"Furze Wren," 97.
Gadwall, 195.
Game Birds, 146-157.
Gannet, 188.
Garden Warbler, 92.

Garganey, 196.
Geese, 189.
"Goatsucker," 127.
Goldcrest, 115.
Golden Plover, 169.
Goldfinch, 64
Goosander, 196.
Goshawk, 129.
"Gowk," 120.
Grasshopper Warbler, 96.
Great Crested Grebe, 216.
Great Tit, 113.
Grebes, 214-217.
Green Cormorant, 187.
Greenfinch, 61.
"Green Linnet," 61.
Green Plover, 167.
Greenshank, 182.
"Grey Crow," 44.
"Grey Duck," 191.
"Greyfowl," 149.
Greyhen, 149.
Grey Wagtail, 53.
Grouse, 147.
Guillemot, 209.
Gulls, 197-202.
  Black-headed, 200.
  Common, 201.
  Great Black-backed, 202.
  Herring, 198.
  Kittiwake, 201.
  Lesser Black-backed, 199.
"Half-curlew," 182.
"Half-duck," 192.
Harriers, 130.
Hawfinch, 58.
Hawks, 129-131.
"Heather Bleater," 180.
"Heather Lintie," 66.
Hedge Accentor, 84.
Hedge Sparrow, 84.
Hen Harrier, 130.
Heron, "Heronsewe," 184.
Herring Gull, 198.
"Hill Blackbird," 76.
Hobby, 133.
Hooded Crow, 44.
"Hoolet," 135.
"Horned Owl," 138.
House Sparrow, 60.
House Martin, 105.
Jackdaw, 39.

Jay, 42.
Kentish Plover, 182.
Kestrel, 134.
Kingfisher, 122.
Kite, 129.
Kittiwake, 201.
Landrail, 158.
Lapwing, 167.
Larks, 46-48.
"Laverock," 46.
Lesser Whitethroat, 91.
Linnet, 65.
Little Grebe, 214.
Little Owl, 140
Long-eared Owl, 138.
Long-tailed Tit, 109.
Magpie, 40.
Mallard, 191.
Manx Shearwater, 208.
"Marrot," 209
Marsh Harrier, 130.
Marsh Tit, 112.
Marsh Warbler, 95.
Martins, 105-107.
"Mavis," 72.
Meadow Pipit, 50.
Merganser, 196.
Merlin, 132.
Missel Thrush, 74.
Montagu's Harrier, 130.
"Moorcock," 147.
"Moorfowl," 147.
"Moorhen," 162.
"Moor-poots," 147.
"Moss-cheeper," 50.
"Nettle-creeper," 90.
Nightingale, 78.
Nightjar, 127.
Norfolk Plover, 166.
Nuthatch, 117.
Osprey, 135.
Owls, 135-141.
"Ox-eye," 113.
Oyster Catcher, 173.
Partridge, 153.
Peewit, 167.
Penguin Tribe, 208.
Peregrine, 132.
Petrels, 207-208.
Pheasant, 150.
Pied Flycatcher, 103.
Pied Wagtail, 52.

GENERAL INDEX.

Pigeons, 142-146.
Pintail, 195.
Pipits, 49-51.
Plovers, 166, 170.
Pochard, 194.
Ptarmigan, 157.
Puffin, 212.
"Pyot," 40.
Quail, 155.
Rails, 157-165.
Raven, 43.
Razorbill, 210.
Red backed Shrike, 108.
Red Grouse, 147.
Red-legged Partridge, 156.
Red-necked Phalarope, 183.
Redpoll, 67.
Redshank, 175.
Redstart, 79.
Red-throated Diver, 213.
Redwing, 75.
Reed Bunting, 70.
Reed Warbler, 94.
Ring Dove, 142.
Ring Ousel, 76.
Ringed Plover or Dotterel, 173.
Robin, 77.
Rock Dove, 145.
"Rock Dove," 144.
"Rock Kestrel," 132.
Rock Pipit, 51.
Rook, 38.
Ruff, 182.
Sand Martin, 106.
Sandpiper, 174.
"Saw-sharpener," 113.
"Scobbie," 63.
"Scoot," 209.
Scoter, 196.
"Screech Owl," 137.
"Sea Mouse," 51.
"Sea Parrot," 212.
"Sea Pie," 173.
"Sea Swallows," 203-207.
Sedge Warbler, 95.
Shag, 187.
Sheldrake, 189.
Short-eared Owl, 139.
Shoveller, 193.
Shrikes, 107-109.
"Shufflewing," 84.
Siskin, 65.

Skuas, 198.
Skylark, 47.
"Smoky," 84.
Snipe, 180.
"Solan Goose," 188.
Song Thrush, 72.
Sparrow Hawk, 131.
"Spink," 63.
"Spoonbill," 193.
Spotted Crake, 161.
Spotted Flycatcher, 102.
Starling, 45.
Stockdove, 144.
Stonechat, 83.
"Stonechat," 80.
Stone Curlew, 166.
"Stormcock," 74.
Storm Petrel, 208.
"Summer Snipe," 174.
Swallow, 104.
Swans, 188.
Swift, 126.
Tawny Owl, 137.
Teal, 192.
Terns, 203-207.
  Arctic, 205.
  Black, 207.
  Common, 204.
  Little, 206.
  Roseate, 206.
  Sandwich, 204.
"Tew-fit," 167.
"Thick-knee," 166.
"Throstle," 72.
Thrushes, 72-98.
"Tit-lark," 50.
Tits or Titmice, 108-117.
Tree Creeper, 116.
Tree Pipit, 49.
Tree Sparrow, 61.
Tufted Duck, 193.
Turtle Dove, 145.
Twite, 66.
Waders, 165-183.
Wagtails, 49, 52-56.
Warblers, 84-98.
"Water Crow," 98.
Waterhen, 162.
"Water Ousel," 98.
Water Rail, 159.
"Whaup," 177.
Wheatear, 80.

Whimbrel, 182.
Whinchat, 81.
"White-rump," 80.
Whitethroat, 90.
White Wagtail, 53.
Wigeon, 195.
Wild Duck, 191.
"Willock," 209
Willow Wren, 85.
"Windhover," 134.
"Window Swallow," 105.

Woodcock, 178.
"Woodcock Owl," 139.
Wood Lark, 48.
"Wood Owl," 137.
Woodpeckers, 118-120.
Wood Pigeon, 142.
Wood Wren, 88.
Wren, 99.
Wryneck, 119.
Yellowhammer, 68.
Yellow Wagtail, 55.

Printed in the United Kingdom
by Lightning Source UK Ltd.
120083UK00001B/69